FIGHTING TIGERS IN ITALY

FIGHTING TIGERS IN ITALY

FIRST HAND ACCOUNTS OF TANKS IN COMBAT

JEFFREY PLOWMAN

Pen & Sword
MILITARY
AN IMPRINT OF PEN & SWORD BOOKS LTD.
YORKSHIRE – PHILADELPHIA

First published in Great Britain in 2025 by
Pen & Sword Military
An imprint of
Pen & Sword Books Ltd
Yorkshire - Philadelphia

ISBN 978 1 39905 786 8

A CIP catalogue record for this book is available from the British Library.

Typeset by SJmagic DESIGN SERVICES, India.

Printed and bound in the UK by CPI Group (UK) Ltd.

The Publisher's authorised representative in the EU for product safety is Authorised Rep Compliance Ltd., Ground Floor, 71 Lower Baggot Street, Dublin D02 P593, Ireland.
www.arccompliance.com

For a complete list of Pen & Sword titles please contact

PEN & SWORD BOOKS LIMITED
George House, Units 12 & 13, Beevor Street, Off Pontefract Road,
Barnsley, South Yorkshire, S71 1HN, England
E-mail: enquiries@pen-and-sword.co.uk
Website: www.pen-and-sword.co.uk

or

PEN AND SWORD BOOKS
1950 Lawrence Rd, Havertown, PA 19083, USA
E-mail: uspen-and-sword@casematepublishers.com
Website: www.penandswordbooks.com

CONTENTS

ACKNOWLEDGEMENTS

I wish to thank the following veterans for their help: Berthold Dölle and Friedrich Huhle (Germany); Ron Biggs, Doug Bull, Ray Curry, Rae Familton, Pat Gourdie, Bruce Grainger, Syd Hemsley, Ben Hobon, Graeme Innes, Lindsay McCully, Jim Moodie, and Pat Stack (New Zealand).

I am grateful to the following for information, photographs, general help, and support: Lee Archer, Michael Benjamin, Peter Brown, Marco Dalmonte, Daniele Guglielmi, Dick Harley, Bob Holt, Brendon O'Carroll, Tony Ormandy, Federico Peyrani, Perry Rowe, Peter Scott, Colin Smith (for the interview with Lindsay McCully), Steve Zaloga, Aidan Dowrick, John Nicholson and Wayne Kaye (for George Kaye's photographs).

My thanks to the following organizations for assistance with information and photographs: the Alexander Turnbull Library (NZ), the Library and Archives of Canada, Narodowe Archiwum Cyfrowe (Poland), the Imperial War Museum (UK), The National Archives (UK), the National Archives and Records Administration (USA), Real War Photos (USA), The Tank Museum (in particular, Stuart Wheeler) (UK), National Army Museum (NZ) and World War Pictures.

Special thanks go to my wife, Yvonne, and our children, Catie and Matthew, for their continued support of me pursuing my hobby of researching and writing military histories.

The archival sources are as follows:

Alexander Turnbull Library (ATL)
Imperial War Museum IWM)

Acknowledgements

Library and Archives of Canada (LAC)
Nardowe Archiwum Cyfrowe (NAC)
National Archives and Records Administration (NARA)
National Army Museum (NAM)
Real War Photos (RWP)
World War Photos (WWP)

INTRODUCTION

Few tanks of the Second World War have inspired the same awe and fear as the Panzerkampfwagen VI (PzKpfw VI) Ausf E, or Tiger I, especially among the soldiers of the Allied armies. But with only 1,347 of them built between August 1942 and August 1944, it was hardly a major tank in the German arsenal when balanced against the Nazi state's total production of 49,777 tanks. By all accounts, the PzKpfw V (Panther), that appeared later, was a much better tank, particularly once its initial issues of reliability were sorted out.

But the Tiger was always the one that stood out. When this 51-ton behemoth first appeared in North Africa in late 1942, it was developmentally far ahead of anything the Allies had. Firing an 88mm round that could pass right through the turret of any tank, and frontal armour virtually impervious to the Sherman tank's main armament of a 75mm, there was little that most Allied tanks could do about it in the open terrain of North Africa. The only Allied tanks that stood a chance against it were the 6-pdr-armed Crusader Mk III and Churchill Mk III. Although a 17-pdr anti-tank gun had made an appearance on a field-mount at this stage of the war, it did not get fitted to the Sherman tank for another eighteen months.

On the negative side, the Tiger was underpowered and its transmission was weak. Indeed, it is likely that more Tigers were lost through mechanical failure than combat in Italy. Worse still, the lack of a good recovery vehicle, until the Bergepanther arrived, meant that crews had to try towing their disabled Tiger back with another Tiger rather than abandon it on the battlefield, often resulting in the loss of both vehicles.

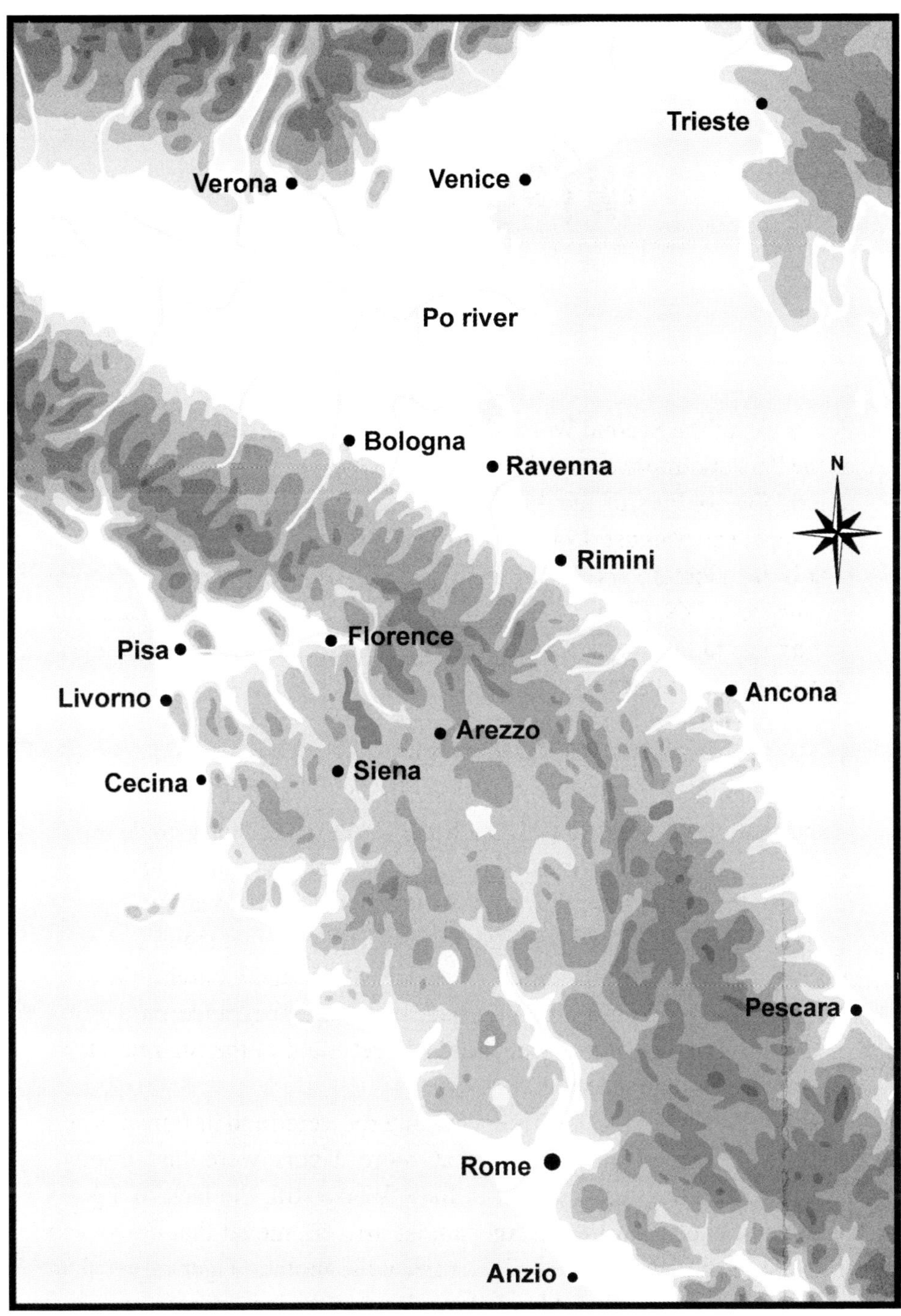

Northern Italy.

Transportation and mobility were also challenges. Delivery to the front line involved transport by rail, but before this could happen the outer set of road wheels had to be removed, followed by the swapping of its battle tracks for narrower transport tracks. Then there were terrain issues. While its wide tracks gave it good mobility off-road, the interleaved arrangement of its road wheels could cause mud, ice or rocks to jam the track mechanism and immobilize the tank, especially in winter when the mud would freeze solid. Under these circumstances, crews had to resort to using blow torches to get the tank mobile again. Tigers were a maintenance nightmare, especially when trying to get access to the inner wheels. Aside from this, many of the bridges in Italy simply could not support the weight of the Tiger.

These issues did not matter to the Allies in Italy, as the Tiger represented a distinct threat that their armour was simply incapable of dealing with. Initial British neglect of tank design and production had seen them slip behind the Germans in this respect. In the US, the 'tank destroyer versus tank' ideology had seen the spawning of two separate lines of armour development, neither of which was in tune with German tank design and armoured tactical doctrine. In fact, the German need to deal with new Soviet armour encountered at longer ranges on the wide-open Russian steppes had led to their progression to higher-calibre and longer-barreled guns, along with larger and heavier armoured tanks and tank destroyers.

Fortunately for the Allied forces, many of these German tanks and tank destroyers did not make their appearance on the Italian field of battle, being more needed elsewhere. Although the Tiger I was an issue for them, it did not appear in sufficient numbers to have a serious impact on operations. Indeed, strategies were developed to deal with them, and on rare occasions the Tiger could be defeated in combat.

Chapter 1

TIGER vs SHERMAN

One of the strict provisos placed on Germany by the Treaty of Versailles at the conclusion of the First World War was a ban on the acquisition of tracked armoured vehicles. Not that this, in any way, stopped the German Heer (Army) from studying the various theories relating to this new addition to modern warfare or developing their own unique approach to it.

Prevented from owning or manufacturing tanks by the 1919 Treaty of Versailles, the German Army instead used these wooden tank mockups on light car chassis for training purposes. (Plowman Collection)

Lacking tanks of their own proved to be no impediment, as wooden mockups of tanks were fitted to ordinary car chassis and used in training exercises. In 1922, to bypass the ban on developing new tanks, Germany went to the extent of establishing a Panzertruppenschule beside the Kama River in Russia in cooperation with the Soviet Union. Here, in secret, over the next seven years they tested new tank designs and developed new tactics of armoured warfare.

This soon changed following the appointment of Adolf Hitler as Chancellor of Germany in 1933, when there was an expansion of the armed services, boosted by the introduction of universal conscription. Simultaneously, as a way of skirting the restrictions of the treaty, Germany launched an ambitious programme with the aim of developing for mass production a range of armoured vehicles. This began with an order for fifteen tank hulls, albeit lacking superstructures, turrets or armaments, these receiving the official designation of 'Landwirtschaftlicher Schlepper', or agricultural tractor. Though destined to serve as training vehicles for the first two Panzer regiments, they formed the basis for Germany's first proper armoured vehicle, the twin machine-gun-armed

One of the first tanks produced by the Germans was the 'Landwirtschaftlicher Schlepper', or agricultural tractor, of which fifteen were produced and used as training vehicles for the new Panzer divisions. (Plowman Collection)

Panzerkampfwagen I, of which 135 were ordered later that year. This was followed by another order for 450 in January 1934. In July that same year, an order was issued for the PzKpfw II, this model to be equipped with a 20mm cannon, capable of firing both high explosive (HE) and armour-piercing (AP) ammunition. Intended primarily for battlefield reconnaissance, it eventually entered production in late 1935, seven months after Hitler's repudiation of the military clauses of the Versailles Treaty on 26 March.

The year 1935 also saw work begin on two new classes of tank for the German Army. The first of these was the PzKpfw III, a 15-ton main battle tank intended for what would become the three medium companies of the Panzer divisions. Unfortunately, it was here that the wishes of senior tank officers parted company with those of the Heereswaffenamt (German Army Weapons Agency). The Panzer officers, knowing that the British were installing the 40mm 2-pdr gun in their tanks, and the latest Russian tanks were rolling off the

This led to the Panzerkampfwagen I (PzKpfw I), of which 818 were produced of the Ausführung A and 675 of the Ausf B. Originally intended for training purposes only, they saw extensive combat service up to and including the invasion of the Soviet Union in 1941. (Plowman Collection)

production line armed with a 45mm gun, wanted the PzKpfw III to be fitted with a 50mm gun.

The Heereswaffenamt, however, argued that as the 37mm anti-tank gun was already on issue to the infantry and in quantity production, it was logical, from the point of view of standardization, that this be fitted to the new tank. In the end, a compromise was reached whereby the tank was to have the 37mm gun but with a turret ring capable of accepting the larger-calibre weapon when the need arose. What resulted from this was a 15-ton vehicle, capable of 25mph, which, for the purposes of security,

For most of the early years of the war, the PzKpfw IV was technically Germany's heaviest operational tank, something that a Soviet delegation found hard to believe when they visited Germany in the spring of 1941. (Plowman Collection)

received the title of Zugführerwagen (platoon commander's vehicle), the first models of which appeared in 1936.

The fourth tank in their new arsenal, the PzKpfw IV, began life as a vehicle intended to suppress enemy anti-tank guns beyond the range of other vehicles with high explosive fire, and for that it was to be equipped with a 75mm L/24 howitzer. The Germans also figured that with a 75mm Panzergranate (armour-piercing shell), it would be capable of defeating some of the heavier French tanks (something that proved not to be the case for the French Char B1 bis and the British Matilda Mk II). Work began on the design of this vehicle in October 1935 under the code name Bataillonsführerwagen (battalion commander's vehicle), the first model of this also appearing in 1936.

Nevertheless, with the spending allocation for armoured fighting vehicles still limited to only 4 per cent of the defence budget, delivery of both the PzKpfw III and IV was slow. This meant that when Germany went to war against Poland on 1 September 1939, the bulk of the tanks in their new Panzer divisions were of the light category, specifically 1,445 PzKpfw Is and 1,223 PzKpfw IIs, there being only 98 PzKpfw IIIs and 211 PzKpfw IVs available in the medium tank category. What saved the Germans were the tanks they had acquired after their annexation of Czechoslovakia, namely 202 PzKpfw 35(t) and 78 PzKpfw 38(t) vehicles, both equipped with a 37mm cannon.

In the end, the PzKpfw I and II did not prove equal to the task, but with the slow production of their two main battle tanks, the Germans had little choice but to continue with them in service until more of the other models became available. In turn, the first two models gradually disappeared from the German arsenal through the process of attrition.

Experience in Poland revealed other inadequacies of the new German steeds. While the poor armour protection of the PzKpfw II could be easily overcome by bolting on extra frontal armour, this could not be achieved on the PzKpfw III without strengthening its suspension. The inadequacy of the weapon of the PzKpfw III in the Polish campaign and that in the Low Countries and France in 1940 was another matter.

With the feeling that a 37mm gun could no longer be relied upon as an armour-defeating weapon, Hitler personally gave instructions in August 1940 that future models of the PzKpfw III be fitted with the 50mm L/60 gun. The problem was that the German armoury also included the less powerful 50mm L/42 gun, and it was this weapon that was installed instead. As General Heinz Guderian, the German Army's foremost advocate of armoured warfare, related, this all came to a head around the time of Hitler's birthday:

> 'Hitler attended a demonstration of armoured equipment on the 18th of April at which I was present. It was on this occasion that he noticed that the Panzer III had been re-equipped by the Army Ordnance Office with a 50-mm L42 cannon instead of with a 50-mm L60 as he had ordered. This independent act on the part of the Ordnance Office infuriated him all the more since it involved a weakening of his original intentions.'[1]

By this stage of the war, plans were well advanced for the invasion of the Soviet Union, codenamed Operation Barbarossa, the success of which was anticipated with much confidence by the German Army. After a visit in the spring of 1941 by a Soviet delegation led by Ivan Tevosian, the Minister of Black Metallurgy, to inspect German tank factories,[2] Guderian had misgivings:

> 'One curious incident made me at least slightly dubious concerning the relative superiority of our armoured equipment. In the spring of 1941 Hitler had specifically ordered that a Russian military commission be shown over our tank schools and factories; in this order he had insisted that nothing be concealed from them. The Russian officers in question firmly refused to believe that the Panzer IV was in fact our heaviest tank. They said repeatedly that we must be hiding our newest models from them, and complained that we were not carrying out Hitler's order to show them everything. The military commission was so insistent on this point that eventually our manufacturers and Ordnance Office officials concluded: "It seems that the Russians must already possess better and heavier tanks than we do."'

This was something the Germans would not discover for sure until they invaded the Soviet Union in June of that year.

In fact, the Germans did have heavier tanks than this, one of which the Russians would have been aware. This was the Neubaufahrzeug, a multi-turreted tank, the concept of which was in vogue at the time. Developed in 1933, two mild-steel and three armoured versions were built. In April 1940, the armoured models were shipped to Oslo for deployment in the invasion of Norway, though mainly for propaganda purposes.

Work on other heavy tank designs had also been underway, starting in January 1937 with the development of a 30-ton Durchbruchwagen I (breakthrough vehicle). Intended to be fitted with 50mm-thick armour and mounting the 75mm L/24 gun, the chassis design was given to

The only heavy tank the Germans possessed at the start of the Second World War was the Neubaufahrzeug, of which the three armoured production models were shipped over to Olso during the invasion of Norway in April 1940. (Plowman Collection)

the firm of Henschel and turret design to Krupp. This progressed to the Durchbruchwagen II, with heavier armour, both vehicles being completed as test chassis with no turrets.

On 9 September 1938, the Heereswaffenamt authorized Henschel to continue work on a tank in the 30-ton class with the same level of armour protection and gun, under the designation VK 30.01. This resulted in a tank with a torsion bar suspension incorporating interleaved road wheels, the first of its type. Four of the six intended prototypes were eventually completed. However, the turrets, though assembled, were never fitted, and in 1944 these were released and installed in the Atlantikwall and Westwall.

To complicate matters, in mid-1939, Krupp was asked to design a new turret with 100mm of armour capable of mounting a 105mm L/20 or L/28 gun for a vehicle projected to weigh no more than 80 tons. Following the fall of France in June 1940, plans for the new tank changed to one of no more than 30 tons because of bridge weight restrictions in that country. Nevertheless, by the end of the design stage, the weight of the Henschel-designed tank had crept up to 36 tons, resulting in its designation being changed to VK 36.01. In May 1941, there was a further change because of the need for a higher penetration weapon, which led to the rescinding of the 105mm L/28 weapon in favour of a 75mm taper bore gun firing tungsten armour-piercing rounds. The resulting vehicle, with 100mm of frontal armour and 60mm-thick side armour, had now increased to 40 tons. Eventually, this project was cancelled too, a major factor being the limited supplies of tungsten in Germany.

A further complication came in the form of a competitor to Henschel, up until then the main German manufacturer of the new heavy tank chassis. Towards the end of 1939, Dr Ferdinand Porsche was given the task of developing a new heavy tank in the 25–30-ton class, incorporating either the existing 75mm L/24 or the new 105mm gun. By March 1941, work on this was sufficiently advanced for the firm to be awarded a contract to manufacture one chassis, the VK 30.01 (P). By this stage, there had been a further change to the weapon to be carried by the new heavy tanks; it was now to be the 88mm L/56 gun. As part of this process, Krupp was given a contract to design a turret capable of mounting the new weapon. This ultimately resulted in a heavier tank, the VK 45.01 (P), the armour for which was also to be manufactured by

Krupp. In July 1941, Henschel was also informed that their tank design had to incorporate this new Krupp turret. This forced them to modify their chassis and resulted in a weight increase to 45 tons and a new designation, the VK 45.01 (H), three prototypes of which were to be assembled for evaluation.

If the Russians were aware of these developments, they showed no sign. Nor were German commanders of the forces about to invade Russia aware of what tanks the Russians had been working on. The Oberkommando des Heeres (OKH, Army High Command) had heard about the production of a new Russian tank, but chose to withhold this information from their tactical commanders.[3]

This Soviet development was based on the 'Bystrokhodny Tank' (BT, fast tank) series, the suspension of which was designed by American inventor J. Walter Christie. These lightly armoured but well-armed tanks had been produced in large numbers between 1932 and 1941, but Russian experiences in the Spanish Civil War and against the Japanese Army in the Far East had shown vulnerabilities in their design. Notably, the armour of the BTs could be easily penetrated by the German 37mm gun, while they proved vulnerable to catastrophic fires through their petrol engines igniting after the tank was hit by artillery or mines.

To overcome these issues, the Russians had turned to developing a replacement for the BT series, with the official designation of T-34. This new tank, while retaining the Christie suspension of the BT series, differed from them with its wider tracks to better negotiate the terrain in Russia, and a diesel engine to reduce its propensity for engine fires. The innovation of the first model of this series, the T-34/76, was the move to angle the armour to 60° on the hull front, 45° on the hull side and 52° on the turret side, thereby effectively doubling its armour thickness. To this tank the Russians fitted a 76.2mm gun. The result was a potent fighting machine, though one whose effectiveness was somewhat diminished by its poor internal layout and Russian organizational ineptitude.

At the time of the German invasion of the Soviet Union, only 12 per cent of the ammunition required by the tank was available, most T-34/76s going into action with less than a full load, and only high explosive rounds at that. This problem also dogged the new Russian heavy tanks, the Kliment Voroshilov (KV) series, which arose out of the desire to build a single-turreted version of one of their heavy

The tank that changed it all for the Germans in the Soviet Union was the T34/76, this particular model being the earliest version produced. (Plowman Collection)

multi-turreted tanks. The result was the KV-1, fitted with the same gun as the T-34/76, and the KV-2, with a 152mm howitzer in a larger turret, both with armour twice as thick as the T34/76.

It was the appearance of these new tanks shortly after the launch of Operation Barbarossa on 22 June 1941 that came as a distinct shock to the invading German forces. On the second day of the operation, a solitary unidentified tank sat across the supply lines of 6. Panzer-Division and destroyed twelve of their trucks. Attempts to eliminate it with a battery of 50mm anti-tank guns failed, even after they closed to a range of just 600 metres. These guns were easily disposed of by the Soviet tank, along with an 88mm gun that was later brought up. The Germans eventually managed to draw its attention away with an attack by some light tanks. Meanwhile, a second 88mm gun was set up, three rounds being needed to knock out the Soviet tank. Even then, its crew refused to abandon their vehicle, only being persuaded to leave when some stick grenades were poked through one of the holes in its armour.[4] From a subsequent examination of the tank, the Germans realized that they had been up against a KV-1.

One of the first encounters with the T-34/76 occurred near the Lithuanian capital of Vilnius, where Russian tanks clearly outmatched the PzKpfw 38(t) models of the Germans, while infantry units elsewhere could only watch on in horror as the tanks attacked them:

> 'A completely unknown type of tank appeared before us. We opened fire immediately, but the armour was not penetrated until the range was 100 metres.'[5]

This would have led to more serious consequences if the inexperienced Russian crews had been able to use the tank effectively. There were also very few such tanks available at this stage of the war (967 out of a total of 19,221 Russian tanks), at least a quarter of which fell into German hands in an enormous pocket in the Belarus region. Other units equipped with these tanks could be driven off by attacks from the air, where the Luftwaffe achieved superiority.

Nevertheless, what followed was a scramble to find an effective way to deal with this new threat. One of these paths led to the development and production of the PzKpfw V Panther, but this would not appear until mid-1943. What was required now was a tank that could deal with the T-34. One solution was to up-gun the PzKpfw III with the 50mm L/60 gun, starting the Ausführung J. The first of these new tanks reached the front line towards the end of 1941. Up-gunning the PzKpfw IV took a little longer. Initial plans called for it to be fitted with the same gun, but when its turret ring proved capable of accommodating much greater recoil than its existing gun, the decision was made to install the 75mm KwK 40 L/43 weapon. These did not reach the front until early 1942.

Meanwhile, work continued apace on the development of the VK 45.01 heavy tank. In 1942, Henschel and Porsche rolled out their prototypes. Porsche's first one, the VK 45.01 (P), was ready in April for a demonstration at Hitler's birthday celebration. It had 100mm of armour on the hull front, 80mm on the sides and rear, 25mm on the deck and 20mm of belly armour, while motive power was provided by a petrol-electric drive train. Confident of acceptance, Porsche also set in motion production of this tank, ordering 100 in total, all of which were completed before manufacture was halted in October.

Henschel's prototype, the VK 45.01 (H), when it finally appeared in April 1942, differed considerably from its Porsche rival, the sides of its superstructure being extended out over the tracks to create sponsons to accommodate the Krupp turret. With the transmission and running gear coming from one of their earlier projects, only the Maybach HL210 engine was new. The decision as to which model to accept was ultimately made between 26 and 31 October, the Tiger-Kommission settling on the Henschel version. Of the Porsche Tigers that were produced, ninety were eventually converted to the Panzerjäger Tiger (P), also known as the Ferdinand, and the rest to either an armoured recovery vehicle (a total of three), a ram tank or training vehicles.

As for the Henschel Tiger, the first production model was completed and shipped to Kummersdorf for testing on 17 May 1942. Thereafter, problems encountered with its brakes and steering gear caused production delays. Manufacturing eventually began, and by the end of the war the total number made had reached 1,347 tanks.

The first production models finally saw action on 29 August 1942, when four of them from 1. Kompanie, schwere Panzer-Abteilung

The Tiger saw its debut around Leningrad on 29 August 1942, and later that year in Tunisia, this one being encountered by the Americans in November. (RWP)

501 were committed in an attack near Leningrad, though it was hardly an auspicious debut. After some initial success in pushing the Russians back, three of the Tigers became disabled, one with a broken drive shaft and the other two with either engine or transmission failure. The only redeeming feature of their debut was that all three were recovered that night without the Russians realizing what they had been facing.

⊙ ⊙ ⊙

As it turned out, the situation regarding armoured vehicles was no less chaotic in Britain. Having led the world in tank design and tactical handling during the First World War and until shortly afterwards, British efforts in both areas started to lag behind those of the Germans. One of the few positive aspects of British tank design over this period was the development of good fighting compartments with turret baskets and power traverse for their turrets, along with two-way radios and crew intercoms.

The Germans had done this too, but had taken it one stage further, building both the PzKpfw III and PzKpfw IV on a modular design to meet future needs. Thus, these tanks could be adapted to fit more powerful guns or have part of their superstructure replaced to convert them into assault guns, self-propelled artillery or other specialized armoured vehicles.

One thing both countries did have in common was the need to transport tanks by rail, this defining the width of the tank, the size of the turret ring and, ultimately, the size of gun it could carry. The British, in their use of a narrower rail gauge, were more constrained than the Germans on the size of gun their tanks could mount. Here, the German concept of moving the superstructure of the Tiger out over the tracks was novel in that it allowed for a larger turret ring and hence a larger-calibre gun. At the same time, their use of interleaved road wheels not only improved performance off-road, but for transport purposes the outer set of road wheels could be removed, along with the track guard covers and its battle tracks replaced by narrower transport tracks. It was a further complication when tanks had to be moved, but it worked.

For the British, a further constraint came from their Road Traffic Act of the 1930s which penalized haulers that exceeded 2.5 tons, production going to lightweight lorries, and hence smaller engines. This had an impact on the engines available to British tanks. There also seemed to be a tendency for the British to order tanks straight from the drawing board, which resulted in them becoming an assemblage of already available components. By 1939, when new tanks were coming online, there was still no mass production, orders often being issued to firms with no previous experience in tank production.

While more funds became available that year, there were not enough new designs to absorb the increase, so money went into expanding the production of existing designs. However, few of these stood the test of time. The final straw in the saga came in April 1940, when the British War Cabinet Committee sent out the following instruction: 'Tank production must not be interfered with either by the incorporation of improvements to the approved types or by the production of newer models.'[6]

In the 1930s, British tank policy underwent a reversal from employing medium tanks, for both supporting infantry and as a substitute for horsed cavalry, to one of separate classes of tanks: light, cruiser and infantry, with the light models replacing the role of the cavalry. The cruiser tank was originally conceived as a replacement for the British light tank, but the first models – the multi-turreted A9 and its successor, the A10 – were hardly that, the latter even being redesignated as a heavy cruiser. The only redeeming feature of both tanks, other than their gun, was their 'slow motion' suspension, later successfully used in the Valentine tank. In Greece in 1941, 3 Royal Tank Regiment lost almost their entire complement of A10s to mechanical failures of one sort or another.

The primary weapon for both the cruiser and infantry tanks was the 2-pdr anti-tank gun, and even though a high explosive round had been manufactured for it, only the armour-piercing round was ever issued to combat units using tanks with this gun. This was probably because the amount of high explosive carried in the 40mm round was considered insufficient to be effective. On the surface, the issue of this gun to their infantry tanks did not make sense, but the British thinking was that they were primarily intended to deal with enemy armour. They considered that it was the job of artillery to support the infantry assault with high explosive fire. In practice, it never worked that way.

The result of this muddle was that the British were left with only around 2,000 tanks by the time they entered the war, of which 300 were mostly obsolete, while the bulk of the rest were light tanks of little combat value.[7] These included only a couple of the 2-pdr Matilda Mk II tanks,[8] the rest of the infantry tanks all being the next-to-useless Mk I version armed only with a machine gun. By this stage, however, a number of the new model of cruiser tanks had become available, the A13 from Nuffield, with running gear based on the Christie-type suspension. While its new suspension worked well, the A13's reliability was poor, due to it being powered by a First World War-era Liberty engine. The cruiser tank that followed it, the Covenanter, suffered from cooling issues and never saw combat, although over 1,700 were built. Its replacement, the Crusader, did see service in North Africa but also had problems with engine cooling that were not cured until 1942, and this by New Zealand engineers.[9]

Like the Germans, the British were also slow to upgrade their primary tank weapon with a more powerful replacement, but for different reasons. There was an acceptance shortly before the evacuation of British troops from Dunkirk in late May and early June 1940 that the 2-pdr anti-tank

The pinnacle of British cruiser tank design in 1941 was the Crusader tank, such as this Mk I. Though sleek-looking and fast, it suffered from mechanical issues. (Plowman Collection)

gun was only just good enough. By the summer of that year, the new British 6-pdr anti-tank gun was ready to go into production, but only if it did not interfere with the production of 2-pdr guns, as there was a need to make up for losses after the fighting in France. Yet as the year progressed, the demand for the 6-pdr only increased. It was here that another issue arose. It turned out that the requirements differed for fitting the guns to a tank or a field piece, but no clear policy emerged as to the number of each required. By the close of 1941, some 300 6-pdr anti-tank guns had been delivered to the British Army, but no tanks were ready to receive them so they were fitted to field carriages. In the end, the Crusader tank turret was modified to take the 6-pdr, but it was not until July 1942 that 100 of them were available for dispatch to the Middle East. Consequently, it was not surprising that the British turned to the US for tanks.

The Americans would have continued along the same lines as the British, but soon realized, from the fighting in Poland and France, that their 37mm gun was fast becoming obsolete; what they really required for their tanks was a gun in the 75mm class. This led to the cancellation of the order for their next tank design, the M2A1 Medium, and its replacement by an order for 1,000 of a new tank, the design specifications for which had only been issued in June 1940. At this point they came up with a different solution. Before the war, the Americans had developed a larger tank for their 37mm gun, the M2 Medium, though it also had four machine guns in sponsons set in each corner of the hull. However, there was an interesting variation of the prototype of this tank, the T5E2, which had a 75mm pack howitzer in the hull on the right and a rangefinder replacing the turret on top.

What finally emerged was the M3 Medium tank that, though ostensibly based on the T5E2 Medium, owed its appearance more to the French Char B1 bis, having its 75mm gun in a barbette on the right, with a 37mm gun in a turret on the left. Therein lay its real problem – its height – for even without the commander's cupola on the turret, this was excessive, the tank needing to expose most of its hull in order to fire the main gun. It also had a large crew, with two sets of gunners and loaders for its guns, plus a driver, radio operator and commander. The British required tanks urgently but were unhappy with the turret of this new tank, which they had dubbed the General Lee. The Americans redesigned the turret, creating a large bustle for the radio and replacing the cupola with a circular hatch. Fitted to the hull, the tank became known to the British as the General Grant. The first pilot version was completed in March 1941, production models following two months later, with the first production models reaching Britain in August of that year. Thereafter, an increasing number were shipped to England and thence to the Middle East.

They came with the US uncapped M72 AP-T armour-piercing round, which the British discovered, to their horror, shattered on the face-hardened plate of a captured PzKpfw III. Fortunately, when the Germans withdrew from Gazala in Cyrenaica, they left behind nearly 20,000 75mm K.Gr.rot.Pz. APC rounds for the 75mm L/24 gun of their PzKpfw IV. The British discovered that, with minor modifications, they could fit this ballistic capped projectile into the M72 shell case, which gave their new steeds an effective weapon against German armour.[10]

Next to be received by the British was the M3 Medium tank, this version, the General Lee, being used for training by US units in England. The British version had a different turret and was known as the General Grant. (WWP)

The first US tank received by the embattled British forces in North Africa was their M3 Light tank, or the General Stuart, more commonly known as a 'Honey'. (Peter Brown)

Initially, though, what the British actually received was the M3 Light tank (known in British service as the General Stuart), following the ratification of the Lend Lease Act between Britain and the US in April 1941. This tank proved to be mechanically sound and fast, the only downside being its radial aircraft engine that used high octane fuel, giving it a short range and a tendency to backfire on start-up and to set fire to itself. Fitted with the US 37mm gun, it had a weapon with equivalent performance to the British 2-pdr but with the added advantage of firing high explosive and cannister shells. Unfortunately, much less thought had gone into the design of the fighting compartment, the tank lacking the turret basket of British tanks. Instead, the crew was forced to clamber over the drive shaft and onto boxes as the turret traversed. Worse still, the turret traverse hand wheel was on the loader's side of the turret and inaccessible to the commander/gunner. For fine control, once semi-aligned, the commander did have a rack and pinion gear to shift the gun around on its gimbal mount. There was also no provision for a radio in the tank, owing to the inclusion of a fixed machine gun in each sponson. Instructions for the driver could only be provided by tapping or kicking his shoulders. The British overcame some of these difficulties by employing the spare driver as the gunner after transferring the traverse gear to the gunner's side of the turret. They also installed a radio in one of the sponsons, but this meant limiting the turret traverse to just from side to side to avoid the leads getting wrapped around the legs of the crew.

While the Grant tank, upon arrival, went some way towards evening up the odds, the problem and frustration for the British was the slowness of the Americans in developing a fully traversing turret in a medium tank. Designated as the T6 Medium, this had started as a project for the US Armored Force, but it took time, their Ordnance Department lacking the capacity to design both this model and the M3 Medium. Aware of this development, the British went so far as to purchase 1,500 of the new model, paying for an extension to the Lima Locomotive Works within which the new tanks were to be built.

Despite this, and almost as an insurance policy, they turned to the Canadians with a view to obtaining a tank based on American automotive expertise that mounted a gun of their requirements. The result was the Ram I, admittedly fitted with a 2-pdr at the time the first mockup appeared in March 1941, a month before the mockup of the T6 was unveiled at Rock Island Arsenal in the US. Curiously, this bore a strong resemblance to the Ram, even down to the escape hatches in the sides of the sponsons over the tracks, though this would seem to be coincidental. The Canadians eventually produced some 2,000 of these tanks, of which 1,899 were the Ram Mk II with its 6-pdr gun.

The US T6 became the M4 Medium tank (General Sherman in British service), the first one off the production line being the cast-hull M4A1 Medium (or Sherman II in British service). In the end, the Americans reneged on their deal, and the British did not get the 1,500 tanks they had pre-purchased, an equivalent number of Grant tanks being dumped on them instead. To make matters worse, the Americans then had the temerity to charge future shipments of the Sherman to the British against the lend-lease credit account they had with them.

The British eventually received 300 Sherman IIs, but only after they had been forced back to El Alamein in Egypt and the situation in the Middle East turned against them. From this humble beginning, a total of 5 different versions of the Sherman were built, with total production reaching 30,346.[11]

The first model of the Sherman to see service in the British Army was the cast-hull M4A1 (British designation Sherman Mk II), followed later by the welded-hull M4, such as this one after being unloaded in Oran. Its height was a result of the need to accommodate a 9-cylinder radial aircraft engine. (Plowman Collection)

With the Sherman, the British got an armoured vehicle with a turret-mounted 75mm gun able to fire an HE round alongside AP. Although it still had a high profile, a consequence of its 9-cylinder radial petrol engine, at least the crew was now back to five. While it did not offer parity with the Germans, it at least gave the British something better than they previously had. The battlefield reality was that the Sherman took a long time to reach equivalence with the PzKpfw IV, and that had a lot to do with the American philosophy at the time.

Like the British, the Americans seemed reluctant to replace its gun with something of better anti-tank capability, this in part due to their belief that tanks should not engage other tanks. They saw this role as being more appropriate for their tank destroyer force, for which they produced a number of vehicles, ranging from the 75mm-armed M3 Gun Motor Carriage, through the M10 Tank Destroyer, with its main armament being a 76mm gun, to the M36 Tank Destroyer, with its 90mm. The problem with all of these was that they were lightly armoured and open-topped, the latter resulting in them being vulnerable to artillery and mortar fire. In time, the Americans learned, as the British had before them, that the best defence against a tank was another tank.

The Allies did develop their own answer to the Tiger, but these arrived late in the war in northwest Europe and well after the appearance of the Tiger's bigger cousin, the Tiger II, or Konigstiger (King Tiger), which first fought during the latter phase of the Normandy campaign. The American response to the Tiger appeared much later in the form of the T26E3 Pershing, the first twenty of which were shipped to Antwerp in January 1945, almost too late for the war. As it turned out, this tank had been first offered to the US Army in January 1944 during a demonstration of tanks at Tidworth in Wiltshire.[12] At the end of the display of the current US tank inventory, a film was shown of this new tank, which was enthusiastically received by many field officers present, including Brigadier General Maurice Rose, who had led a combat command of the US 2nd Armored Division in North Africa. The underlying problem was old thinking in the military hierarchy rather than technical or financial issues. Lieutenant General George Patton, the highest-ranked US armoured commander in the European theatre, was totally against the new tank, still being locked in the old philosophy that tanks were not meant to fight tanks. As a result, Supreme Headquarters Allied Expeditionary Force (SHAEF) notified Washington DC to 'de-emphasise' production of the Pershing!

The British solution was the A34 Comet, a development of the A27 Cromwell, but mounting a 77mm gun, essentially a 17-pdr gun firing ammunition with a lower charge than that of the standard 17-pdr. There were enough available to equip an entire armoured brigade, but this process was interrupted by the German assault through the Ardennes in late 1945 and the tank did not see service until the final month of the war.

To resolve the issue, the Americans contented themselves with up-gunning the Sherman. Initial experiments in the US involved fitting the 76mm gun into the turret of a standard Sherman, but after receiving complaints that it restricted movement in the turret, they turned to fitting the turret of the experimental T23 tank to the standard Sherman.

The British, however, chose to install their 17-pdr anti-tank gun directly into the standard Sherman turret, turning it sideways for ease of loading ammunition. In addition, they moved the radio back into a box welded to the turret bustle at the rear to create room for the gun and its recoil. It was an odd solution but it worked.

Both these tank models were first deployed in Normandy, where the 17-pdr version was known as the Sherman Firefly. It would be several months after that before these tanks reached the Italian theatre.

Chapter 2

ANZIO TO ROME

In January 1943, a high-level conference to discuss the next phase of the war was held in Casablanca, Morocco, between US President Franklin D. Roosevelt and the British Prime Minister, Winston Churchill. At this stage, the Americans were strongly in favour of a direct assault on the beaches of northwest Europe. However, their mobilization and industrial production had not yet reached a stage where they were in a position to do so. Nor were the British. The abortive Canadian seaborne assault of Dieppe in 1942 had shown them how ill-prepared the Allies were to carry out amphibious operations on heavily defended beaches of the type likely to be encountered in northern France. Instead, Churchill promoted the idea of the Allies wresting control of the island of Sicily from the Axis, to be followed by an invasion of mainland Italy. The logic for this was that it would pull German reserves down into Italy, where they could not be so easily extracted when the Allies opened the Second Front and landed troops on the beaches of Normandy. Faced with these facts, the Americans reluctantly agreed to this course of action.

Thus, on 9 July, some two months after the conclusion of the campaign in North Africa, the Allies launched their invasion of Sicily, the island being secured six weeks later. This was followed by the landing of British forces at Reggio Calabria on the toe of the Italian mainland on 3 September. The Italian government could see the writing on the wall and signed an armistice with the Allies the same day, although this declaration was not made public for five days.

The German response upon learning of this treachery by the Italians was quick and vigorous. Using what forces they had at their disposal, they took over control of Rome. They also threw what units they had in southern Italy against the main Allied force when it landed at Salerno on 9 September, later sending more reinforcements. By 19 September, with the Salerno beachhead secure, the Allies were finally able to begin their push northwards, making good progress until the rains of autumn arrived and the pace of their advance slowed.

By the end of 1943, the Allies, having started the campaign with no clear strategy, were still not sure as to how to proceed. Immediately ahead lay the Gustav Line, one of the more formidable defensive lines the Germans had set up to guard the Liri Valley, the most direct route to Rome. It was at this point that the possibility of outflanking the Germans with an amphibious landing closer to Rome occurred to the Allied planners, but the time to do this was limited. This was because the Mediterranean theatre of operations would only have access to the landing craft for such

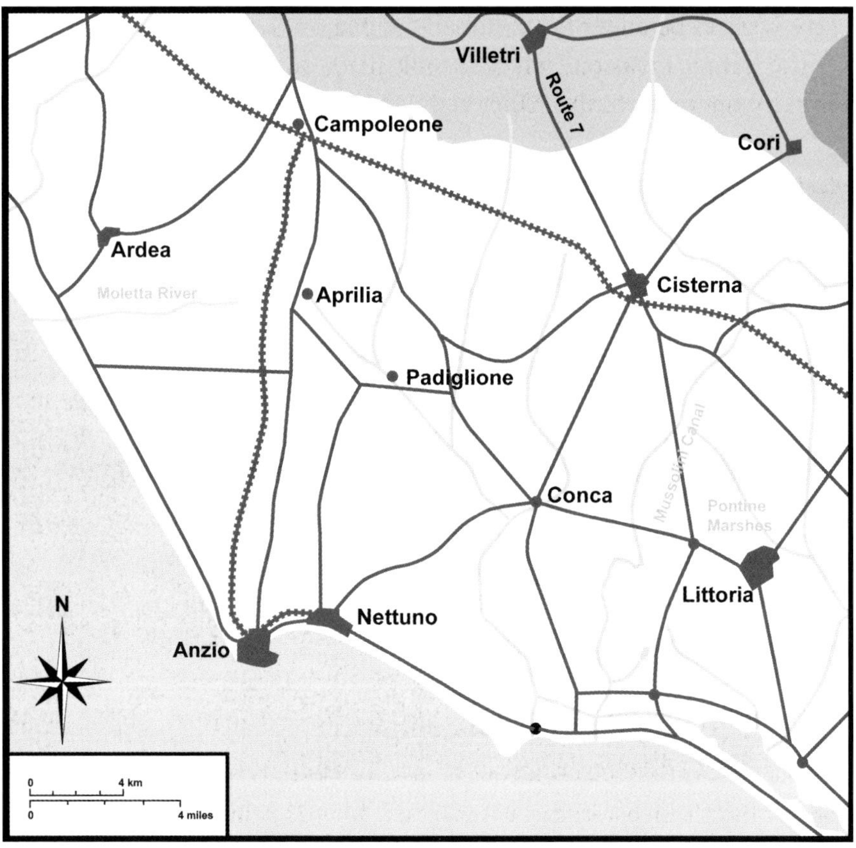

The Anzio-Nettuno battleground.

an operation until the end of January 1944. After this, the craft were to be withdrawn in preparation for a set of landings in southern France to follow on from the main assault in Normandy. It was under these circumstances that Operation Shingle was born, an amphibious assault in the area around Anzio-Nettuno, the intent of which was to outflank the forces along the Gustav Line and enable an attack on Rome.

When finally drawn up, the plans for Operation Shingle called for British forces, primarily the 1st Division and two commando battalions, landing to the northwest of Anzio, and US troops from the 3rd Infantry Division, a US Ranger battalion and an airborne regiment coming ashore to the southeast of Nettuno. Armoured support for these forces was to come in the form of 46 Royal Tank Regiment for the British and the 751st Tank Battalion for the Americans, with the promise of two combat commands of the US 1st Armored Division to follow on later. All of these were to be under the command of Major General John P. Lucas.

The actual invasion, when it took place on 22 January 1944, was virtually unopposed, the Allies only having to deal with some isolated

The first British armour landed at Anzio came from 23 Armoured Brigade, among them this Sherman III from 46 Royal Tank Regiment photographed on 23 January 1944. (IWM)

It soon became evident that tank destroyers were little more than mobile anti-tank guns and should be used to back up infantry once an objective could be taken, this M10 (3-inch) GMC performing such a role behind this haystack near Anzio. (NARA)

shore batteries. A US reconnaissance jeep patrol from the 3rd Infantry Division even reached the outskirts of Rome without encountering any opposition. Nevertheless, by the end of the day, the Allies had landed some 36,000 men and 3,200 vehicles, plus a week's worth of supplies, and established bridgeheads 3–5km inland.

The German response to this threat was immediate. The commander of Army Group C, Generalfeldmarschall Albert Kesselring, ordered what units he could pull together to seal off the Allied landing force, primarily 4. Fallschirmjäger-Division and elements of Panzer Division Hermann Göring, both then near Rome. By nightfall on 22 January, some units from the latter had seized a few bridges on the Allied right flank of the beachhead.

Fortunately for the Germans, the Allies made no effort to push beyond their bridgehead towards the Alban Hills, or even to establish a more defensible perimeter, one that encompassed the key road junctions at Campoleone and Cisterna. Instead, Lucas was more concerned with consolidating what territory the Allies held and building up supplies there. To assist with this, the Fifth Army commander, General Mark

The battle for the Anzio-Nettuno bridgehead saw the first use in Italy of the M18 (76mm) GMC, all with the Reconnaissance Company of the 894th Tank Destroyer Battalion. While still lightly armoured like the M10 GMC, the advantage it offered was its increased agility, a function of its higher speed. (NARA)

W. Clark, sent more troops into the bridgehead, among them the 45th Division, the first elements of which began arriving on 25 January. The need for more armour saw the release of two combat commands from the 1st Armored Division, which started to arrive at the end of the month. Despite this, the Germans were able to move troops into the bridgehead faster than the Allies, very soon outnumbering them, and it was not until 25 January that the balance had shifted back in the other direction.

In the British sector, the 1st Division managed to push the Germans out of the town of Aprilia on 25 January, only to be thrown out themselves the next day. Fortunately for the British, help came in the form of the newly arrived 1st Armored Division under General Ernest N. Harmon.

The first Tigers to be deployed on mainland Italy were from Panzer-Kompanie Meyer, this Tiger being photographed at Anzio at the end of January 1944. (NAC)

With this support, they renewed their attack along the Anzio–Via Anziate road, driving a wedge between 65. Infanterie-Division and 3. Panzergrenadier-Division. Though they were unable to take the rail station at Campoleone, the British did manage to secure a narrow thumb some 6km north of Aprilia. That night in the US sector, the 3rd Division launched a thrust towards Cisterna but only managed to close to within 800 metres of the town, running up against a German counter-offensive that forced them back with heavy losses. This left the Germans with no option but to call off their counter-offensive scheduled for 1 February. Instead, they dug in and strengthened their defences.

It was around this time that the first Tigers reached the Anzio-Nettuno bridgehead, all under the command of Oberleutnant Hans-Gery Meyer of Panzer-Kompanie Meyer. Handily placed in northeastern Italy after its formation on 26 July 1943, it had been sent there over concerns about the deteriorating situation in the Mediterranean. Following shortly after was schwere Panzer-Abteilung 508, a unit that had been formed in August 1943 in Heilbronn, north of Stuttgart, by converting Panzer-Regiment 8 to Tigers. Though the original plans for its deployment were not clear, the Allied landings at Anzio-Nettuno settled the matter, and on 4 February 1944 the unit began its move to Italy, as Hans Becker related:

> 'We detrained in Ficulle at about 09:00 on 10 February. It is about 100 kilometres [north] from Rome. The train couldn't go any further as the bridges were out. The unloading was carried out very quickly and, to my amazement, without interference from enemy aircraft. When I woke again at 07:00 I couldn't believe my eyes, for the landscape was white and the Tigers were covered in snow. It was snowing heavily. By 17:00 in the afternoon the wheeled vehicles were lined up behind the Tigers of the headquarters and the 1st Company. We made our way up the steep serpentines and the Tigers completely wrecked the road. Driving behind the tanks was a shambles. There was about 20cm of snow on the hill and a heavy snowstorm was in progress. We suffered miserably from the cold. Finally, we stopped just outside Orvieto and the wheeled vehicles were sent on their way.'[1]

The needs of the German forces facing the Allies meant that when 1. Kompanie of the unit reached Rome on 12 February, it was immediately sent onwards to the Anzio-Nettuno area, to be joined five days later by 2. Kompanie.

The next to arrive was 1. Kompanie, schwere Panzerjäger-Abteilung 653, under the command of Oberleutnant Helmut Ulbricht. On 15 February they had been issued with eleven Ferdinands, following their complete rebuild after their disastrous deployment the previous year at Kursk on the Russian front. In addition, they had a maintenance platoon with a SdKfz 9/1 halftrack mounting a portable crane and a recovery version of the Ferdinand. They entrained the following day at the Nibelungen Works in St Valentin, Austria, the company eventually reaching Rome on 24 February. Here, they were attached to schwere Panzer-Abteilung 508 and shortly afterwards were ordered forward to the frontline.

On 16 February the Germans launched an attack against the US troops of 45th Division at Carroceto, the fighting centred around the small town of Aprilia, with subsidiary attacks against British and US forces

The next Tiger unit to reach Italy was schwere Panzer-Abteilung 508, these tanks being first deployed in the Anzio bridgehead on 29 February 1944. (RWP)

The fighting around Anzio also saw the first deployment of the Ferdinand tank destroyer of 1. Kompanie, schwere Panzerjäger-Abteilung 653. (Plowman Collection)

on either side. This was soon brought to a halt by the Allies, but was followed up on 29 February by a second assault, Operation Seitensprung (Escapade). This thrust, towards Isola Bella from Carano against US troops from 3rd Division, incorporated a diversionary attack against the British 56th Division on the western shoulder of the salient.

For this attack, the Tigers of 2. Kompanie, schwere Panzer-Abteilung 508 and the Ferdinands of 1. Kompanie, schwere Panzerjäger-Abteilung 653, were combined into Kampfgruppe Stein and sent in on the first morning of the attack. Unfortunately for the Germans, things did not go according to plan, as Oberfeldwebel Hans Bähr, a crewman in one of the Tigers, later wrote:

> 'Our artillery barrage began firing at 0500 hours. At 0700 hours we moved out of the assembly area, single file on a muddy road past Cisterna in the direction of Isola Bella. We were on the edge of the Pontine Marshes, which

> had been drained by Mussolini. The lead tank, commanded by Oberfähnrich Harder, ran onto a mine. While the tank withstood the shock, the leading roadwheel's torsion bar was broken. The tank had to be towed away. … The entire armoured column came to a halt, since none of the other vehicles could pass in that marshy area. Engineers were called up to clear the mines but, for the time being, we had to wait. And then it began. The enemy artillery began ranging in on us. An enemy reconnaissance aircraft circled overhead, maintaining a respectful distance from our anti-aircraft machine guns, but he was directing the artillery fire. A smoke round landed, followed immediately by a salvo of three. … The next day I learned that an artillery round had penetrated the roof of one of our tanks, seriously wounding Obergefreiter Fritz Holwarth, who died later in the evening.'[2]

According to Erich Amann in another Tiger:

> 'The artillery fire became heavier by the minute. The rounds were bursting quite close to us. Shrapnel struck our vehicle. One burst shredded two roadwheels on the right side, and a fragment pierced the stowage box on the back of the turret. By that time it was noon. A suspicious house 1,500 metres in front of us was peppered with high explosive rounds. Enemy infantry ran away. 1400 hours: The enemy fire was unbroken. Then suddenly we were hit twice on the rear of the turret, four of five more hits followed. Two Sherman tanks were firing at us from the right. We immediately returned fire, one Sherman began to burn, the other ran for it. … The Tommies began firing phosphorus rounds, one of which landed in front of the vehicle. Leaking fuel caught fire. We had to get out.'[3]

To add to the woes of Kampfgruppe Stein, some Tigers ran into a minefield under artillery fire and were disabled, their recovery having to wait until nightfall. As it turned out, the tanks referred to above were most probably American, not British, as noted in this combat report of the 751st Tank Battalion:

> '[T]he enemy launched an attack with armor along the road running South from CISTERNA against our positions in vicinity of 0008293 and along the road running Southwest in the vicinity of PONTE ROTTO. One tank was knocked out vicinity of 0006293, hit by A.P. shot from enemy tank. T/5 Alvin G. Probasco was killed in action, Sgt Adam J. Stenger and Pvt William R. Wirsig are missing in action.'[4]

The Germans pushed forward again on 1 March, but their losses the previous day limited their course of action. This time the Tigers were joined by elements of schwere Panzerjäger-Abteilung 653, though it proved to be an inauspicious start for the Ferdinands, as Unteroffizier Heinz Henning and gunner Heinrich Schäfer later described:

> 'Oblt Stein (S.Pz-Abt 508), as was customary in our unit, drove along the road at the point of our attacking tanks. Due to their heavy weights, the Tigers and Ferdinands had to remain on solid roads. Open terrain was too soft. Oblt Stein convinced Uffz. Kühl to take over the point position because of the heavy frontal armour on his Ferdinand. Oblt Stein would secure the flanks with his mobile turret. A destroyed bridge before the town of Isola Bella ended the advance. Uffz. Kühl turned the tank around on the road. The Ferdinand slid off the road and into a ditch with one of its tracks and became stuck. Oblt. Stein wanted to recover the Ferdinand with his Tiger. Both loaders refused to exit their vehicles because of the enemy mortar and artillery barrages. Heinrich Schäfer therefore voluntarily left his vehicle and attached the Ferdinand to the Tiger. The road wheel on the second idler arm was already shot up. Two S-hooks broke during the recovery attempt. All subsequent recovery attempts were illusory, because the non-functional idler arm bent diagonally between the lower track and entire upper track protruding from the hull. It made no difference whether the vehicle attempted to move forwards or

> backwards. A typical Porsche-Tiger ailment. Completely out of breath Heinrich Schäfer reached the crew compartment again and, fortunately for him, collapsed exhausted at the rear of the compartment. A kinetic energy round penetrated the armour on the side of the crew compartment. Uffz Kühl and one of the loaders suffered minor shrapnel wounds. Uffz Kühl gave the order "Abandon vehicle" and all of us hastened back to our front line.'[5]

According to Schäfer, another Ferdinand was also lost that evening:

> 'The same occurred with Feldwebel Gustav Koss' Ferdinand. Feldwebel Koss was on a track about 200 metres parallel to the notorious macadam road. He was a bit further back when he ran over a mine. Uffz Golinski and I were present when a recovery tank, driven by Willi Löffler, attempted to tow the vehicle. I sat forward in the radio operator's position, next to the driver. It was hell, with shells bursting all around us. A dead comrade from the maintenance platoon was laid to rest next to the driver on the track guard cover. This recovery attempt also had to be abandoned. The commander, Oblt Helmut Ulbricht, accompanied by his jeep driver Otto Weller, personally blew up the Ferdinand during a dark night.'[6]

Ultimately, Operation Seitensprung failed, the Allies having expected it and responding with a heavy bombardment after the Germans began their preliminary shelling. The German attack ground to a halt that evening after managing to penetrate some 800 metres into the American lines, leaving them under heavy fire. That night, the Americans counter-attacked and regained the small salient the Germans had taken. With this, the Germans decided to seal off the bridgehead to prevent it expanding further. Then, on 3 March, Panzer-Kompanie Meyer was absorbed into schwere Panzer-Abteilung 508 and the entire unit withdrew to Forte Tiburtino, Rome, and thence to Velletri. There they remained for the next two-and-a-half months.

The tide eventually turned against the German defenders at Anzio-Nettuno when the Allies broke through on the Cassino front on 18 May. Some five days later, with these troops closing in on Anzio, Lucas's replacement at Anzio, Major General Lucian Truscott, launched an attack to break out of the bridgehead. As part of the German effort to counter this, 2. Kompanie, schwere Panzer-Abteilung 508, was brought forward to engage the Americans. Erich Amann recalled:

> 'We reached the railway embankment of the Rome–Naples line. All of the tanks had to pass through an underpass and subsequently assemble in a dispersed formation. Enemy infantry were fired on with high explosive rounds and machine guns. There were also enemy tanks but they were still too far away to be engaged effectively. After advancing three or four kilometres into enemy territory the attack bogged down. The enemy's artillery began firing. We were familiar with that. Leutnant von Werder gave the order to discharge smoke and withdraw. We turned around under cover of the smoke and headed back, our guns in six o'clock position.
>
> 'Our driver failed to see a deep drainage ditch. Thump! We were in it, the engine died. With no servo-assist, Unteroffizier Richter was forced to summon superhuman strength to disengage the clutch in order to shift into neutral. Then a blow against the turret which caused the submachine guns to fall from the racks. An anti-tank hit which failed to penetrate. Thank God!
>
> 'After a few minutes we were through the underpass and on the other side of the embankment, where we were out of the enemy's sight. There was a brief pause in the fighting, perhaps 15 minutes. We were able to climb out and inspect where the shell had struck and stretch our legs a little. The enemy's artillery began firing then. The enemy spotter plane had discovered us just on the other side of the embankment.... Not surprisingly, therefore, we received orders to move. Start engines. Ours refused to start. Unteroffizier Richter checked the engine temperature and read off 120° Celsius.'[7]

Examination of the tank showed that the armour-piercing round had deflected off the turret and downwards onto the radiator's heavy vertical protective vents, past the sloped shield above the fuel tanks and onto the radiator. The company commander was radioed about this and ordered another tank forward to tow it. At this point, as Amann got out of the tank to fetch the tow cables, the disabled Tiger and that of Oberfeldwebel Hans Bähr came under heavy artillery fire. This lasted for half an hour. When one of Bähr's crew was mortally wounded, they threw him into the tank and drove off. This left one other Tiger, that of Feldwebel Kurt Ilmer, at this stage sheltering under the railway bridge. Amann continued his account:

> 'An hour later we were able to connect the tow cables to Feldwebel Ilmer's tank. We didn't get far. After about one kilometre in the soft, moor-like terrain the steel cable, which was about 40 millimetres thick, broke. Only the maintenance company's two 18-ton prime movers could tow us out of this difficult terrain. … The front had grown quiet by then; night had fallen. We decided to let the tow tank continue on its way. The driver and I (the loader) stayed behind with our tank to take turns standing watch through the night. At about 0200 hours the driver noticed that the engine temperature was reading 40° Celsius. … I climbed onto the commander's seat and put on the headset. The motor did in fact start, and we rumbled over the terrain. After 500 metres we had to stop. The thermometer indicated 120°C. But we had established something and were overjoyed. We had to wait four hours and then cover another 500 metres. By then the new day had broken. At every halt we immediately camouflaged the vehicle. … I stood watch in the turret. Toward evening a figure approached. Halt: Who goes there? It was Otto Jahnle of the repair section. He had been looking for us for some time. What did we need? "Bring jerry cans full of water." An hour later he arrived on his Kettenkrad [halftrack motorcycle] with six to eight jerry cans full of the precious liquid. I poured it into the radiator filler point. It flowed

> through the hole, but it cooled the engine and Unteroffizier Richter could drive. Once we reached the road we were able to increase speed. While I kept the engine cool, Otto Jahnle delivered fresh cans of water. After stopping at the company in Velletri, the next day we drove on to Forte Tiburtina [*sic*] in Rome.'[8]

Thereafter, it was a question of the Tigers slowly having to give up ground to the Americans pushing forward, though at some cost to the Allies. That same day, during an attack across the railway embankment at Cisterna-Latina, 2. Kompanie claimed the destruction of fifteen tanks for the loss of one Tiger, though this may have been an over-estimation. The combat report for the 751st Tank Battalion on this day noted the loss of six tanks from Company A from mines and one from anti-tank fire, while Company B lost one tank from anti-tank fire.

On 26 May, Herbert Ströll wrote of another encounter with an American tank battalion that had run up against schwere Panzerjäger-Abteilung 653:

> 'Four o'clock in the morning, a new operation. We stood in the middle of the main road to Cisterna. A sudden radio message, "Enemy tanks!" I loaded my machine gun and peered continuously through the optics. Sweat dripped from my face in the heat. We still did not see any tanks. They drove around us to the left and attempted to surround us. Suddenly the gun commander screamed, "Tank, hurry shoot, shoot!" An American tank emerged onto our road from a defile on the left. We decided his fate in a matter of seconds. The first hit blew him sky high. Three men jumped out as the first flames erupted from the tank. I wanted to shoot him [*sic*], damn it, my machine gun jammed. A Tiger tank half a gun tube in front of us also shot at the tank, but we were faster! Two men from the American crew came forward and surrendered. They approached our tank with raised hands, constantly looking at the machine gun I had aimed at them. I let them live.'[9]

By 2 June, however, the Allies had finally broken through the German defences, with one force advancing over the Alban Hills towards Rome and the other about to cut Route 6 from Cassino. This forced the Germans to abandon their defences and pull back through Rome. The American Fifth Army entered the city on 5 June, just one day before the Allied landings on the beaches of Normandy.

As with the Tiger's debut around Leningrad in 1942, its initiation to combat on mainland Italy at Anzio proved to be less than satisfactory, with several of its deficiencies coming to the fore. Its wide tracks and interleaved road wheels offered no advantages over the Allied tanks in this region of the former Pontine Marshes. Furthermore, with only two Famo 18-ton SdKfz 9 halftracks in the unit for recovery purposes, both of which were needed to tow one Tiger, their only other resort was to tow a disabled Tiger with another. Unfortunately, as they were to discover later, this risked overloading the transmission in the towing tank, leading to the loss of both tanks. On the plus side, the Tiger's frontal armour was impervious to fire from Sherman tanks, there being little opportunity for approaching the Tiger from the flank, the Sherman coming off worse in these encounters. The only other effective option for the Allies was long-range artillery fire, which, despite its inaccuracy, did catch the odd Tiger from time to time.

Chapter 3

THE CECINA TIGER

Whatever Generalfeldmarschall Kesselring's intentions had been after the fall of Rome, a directive from Hitler not to yield a further yard of ground on all fronts put a constraint on his possible courses of action. This meant to Kesselring, at least, that the retreat was to be stabilized along a line running from Grosseto to the mountains, then through Lake Trasimeno to Ancona on the Adriatic, the Albert Line. What he needed was time to complete work further back on the Gothic Line, a major defensive position that ran along the Foglia River between Pesaro and Cattolica on the Adriatic coast, before passing through the Apennine mountain range to La Spezia on the Ligurian coast.

To achieve this, Kesselring had established a series of blocking lines between Rome and the Arno River. Of these, the Dora Line, just to the north of Rome, and the Albert Line itself were reasonably substantial, but two more between them and the Arno were little more than delaying lines. Kesselring also made some adjustments in his troop dispositions, strengthening 14. Armee on his western flank by moving XIV Panzer-Korps to join I Fallshirmjäger-Korps and reinforcing 10. Armee to the east with LXXVI Panzer-Korps.

The reality, though, was that due to earlier losses, Kesselring was in no position to seriously oppose the Allies at this stage. This meant that the Allied armies made rapid progress immediately after the fall of Rome. This soon began to change, with Eighth Army (Lieutenant General Oliver Leese) meeting stiffening resistance as it drove up the Tiber Valley until British troops entered Perugia, east of Lake Trasimeno, on 20 June. Here, their advance was checked by resistance to the north of the town. The following day, the 6th South African Armoured

Division suffered their first reverse in Italy while trying to take Chiusi to the west of the lake. Over on the coast, the Americans seized the port of Civitavecchia on 7 June and the Viterbo airfields two days later. On 12 June, the 36th Infantry Division secured Grosseto. Over on their right flank, Task Force Ramey from 1st Armored Division forced the German defenders out of their strongpoint in Triana. The end result of all this was to place the Americans within striking distance of the Albert Line, only to have their advance brought to a sudden halt when a burst of heavy rainfall turned the land into a morass.

Ahead of the Americans lay the rugged hills of Tuscany, with their steep-sided ridges, a considerable change from the rolling hills south of Viterbo. It was here that General Clark decided to fully commit 1st Armored Division, despite General Harmon's protest that this was no place for tanks, the unit taking over the advance from the 36th Division. The timing could not have been worse because it saw the entry of a second Tiger unit into Italy, schwere Panzer-Abteilung 504. This unit was no stranger to the Mediterranean theatre of operations, 1. Kompanie having fought in Tunisia and 2. Kompanie in Sicily, the latter escaping just in time with its last remaining Tiger. Back in Paderborn, Germany, the unit had been rebuilt from its survivors before being sent to Italy in June 1944. On 20 June, 1. Kompanie was committed to battle in the sector of the Turkmenistan troops of 162. Infanterie-Division, Harmon's armour running into some of their Tigers the following day.

For this phase of the advance, the 1st Armored Division had been operating in three columns: Combat Command A (CCA) on the left, CCB on the right and Task Force Howze in the centre. The latter, under the command of Colonel Hamilton H. Howze, included 13 Armored Regiment, 1st Battalion of 6 Armored Infantry Regiment, Company A of the 701st Tank Destroyer Battalion, with attached engineers, and artillery. On 22 June, CCA had the most success, pushing forward 8km by nightfall. CCB, however, ran into trouble shortly after swinging off Route 1 and turning onto the road to Massa Marittima. Its route passed through a narrow saddle in the hills, and as it crossed the rise it came under fire from nine Tigers. Although CCB claimed to have knocked out several Tigers in the encounter, it was forced to withdraw.

Under orders to relieve pressure on CCB, Howze sent the M5A1 Light tanks of Company B, 13th Tank Battalion, and a platoon of M10 tank destroyers from the 701st Tank Destroyer Battalion 16km back over Route 1 and around to the right. After working their way through some demolitions and mines and encountering slight resistance, they drove out into the open in full view of a platoon of Tigers from 1. Kompanie, schwere Panzer-Abteilung 504, under the command of Oberfähnrich Röhrig. In the ensuing engagement, eleven US tanks and tank destroyers were knocked out and the other twelve abandoned by their crews. These were later destroyed by Röhrig's Tigers.[1]

Task Force Howze, however, did extract partial revenge on 25 June. In the lead on this occasion was an infantry platoon from 361 Infantry Regiment, a platoon of M4 Mediums from Company B, 13th Tank Battalion, and a platoon of M10s. While moving northeast out of Prata towards Montieri, they flushed out some snipers from the woods lining the road, taking several prisoners in the process. According to their report:

> 'After a couple of miles, the armoured vehicles halted in a very deep ravine while the infantry platoon sent out a reconnaissance party to look around the first bend of an

Tigers 200 and 211 from schwere Panzer-Abteilung 504 were destroyed by their crews just to the north of Massa Marittima on 25 June 1944 after being towed there by their crews in the hope that they could be repaired. (Plowman Collection)

S curve. The task force commander arrived at the head of the column in a jeep just as the infantry platoon leader emerged from the woods on the right of the road to report that the column was being held up by a German tank just around the bend. The doubting task force commander verified this report by climbing up through the woods to a [good observation point], focusing captured German field glasses on the road about 30 feet below and 200 yards distant. In the glasses, the enemy tank looked enormous and startlingly near.

'I thought I could reach out and pat it. I swung my vision left along the road and there, looking like another beached 10,000 ton cruiser, was a second Tiger. Both of these creatures had their guns leveled directly at the bend of the road where it rounded the nose [on which I was], and in the turret of each stood the tank commander, visible from the waist up, and clad in black German uniform.'[2]

At this point, under Howze's orders, a platoon of infantry made their way stealthily into position on some high ground flanking the curving road near the tanks. Taking one man with a bazooka with him, the platoon commander then joined Howze at his observation post. At the same time, using the high grass and brush in a creek bottom for cover, the commander of the tank destroyer platoon conducted a brief reconnaissance through to the left of the road and determined the exact location of the first Tiger.

Howze's plan called for the bazooka operator to fire at one of the Tigers, this being the cue for the platoon to pour small-arms fire onto both. Once he heard the infantry commence firing, the leading M10 was to wait thirty seconds, drive around the bend and open fire on the lead Tiger. At the same time, the commander of the point tank, Lieutenant Carl Key, was to follow the M10, come alongside it, and engage whatever target he could see.

Howze later related what happened when the simple plan was put into operation:

'I watched the German tanks with all the happy anticipation with which a bird watches a cobra; again and again

> I expected the guns to come suddenly alive, swing their big noses up, and blow us off the hill. The leading tank commander appeared nervous and suspicious, for he frequently raised his binoculars to his eyes and peered up into the woods on his immediate left, and once he directed his glasses almost exactly on the point where I was sitting, and we seemed to stare fixedly at one another for a long half-minute. The rest of the German crewmen were likewise upset or apprehensive. … It was a long and trying time for us, getting ready, but finally the platoon leader announced he was set. I took a long breath and told him to open fire.
>
> 'The bazooka gunner had used the delay to take very careful aim. His first shot was a direct hit on the front plate of the leading tank, remarkable at 200 yards. The crew had just buttoned up the turret. The projectile did not penetrate but did explode with a loud crash. The infantry platoon fired all its weapons, although one more bazooka projectile actually hit the tank. Dust and smoke obscured the second tank but the first could be seen maneuvering to get out of a shallow roadside ditch onto the macadam. Its big gun never blasted at the hillside, and its movements were lumbering and awkward.'[3]

The tank destroyer remained under cover and motionless until Colonel Howze scrambled down to it and forced the driver to execute his earlier orders. The command tank of Lieutenant Carl Key went around the bend behind the M10 and branched off to the left across a small bridge leading to a good firing position on the flank opposite the infantry. From there it repeatedly hit the leading Tiger tank but without penetrating its armour. Nevertheless, the Germans became panicky and tried to climb out and escape, whereupon the infantry platoon cut them down.

A small group of buildings at the minehead occupied the small flat area from which Key's tank was firing. A galvanized-iron, hangar-like warehouse with wide, swinging doors ajar at each end stood between the tank and part of the road limiting Key's field of fire. A considerable stretch of the road was visible, however, through the far door, and when the first Tiger had been abandoned, Key had his M4's gun swung to the left, and fired a few rounds through the shed along the road in the hope of blocking off the second tank. The result was an outstanding racket, a cloud of thick dust in the shed and some blind shooting. After a few minutes, all firing ceased. No enemy tank was visible except the abandoned monster.

Exactly what happened to the second Tiger was not recorded, but when members of the task force visited the area several days later, they found another Tiger that had thrown its track in mud, the result of two damaged bogies. There was also evidence of it having been struck by 75mm projectiles.

Over the next five days, 1st Armored Division, led by CCB, continued northwards through the towns of Gerfalco, Monterotondo, Fosini, Castelnuovo and Pomarance, ultimately crossing the Cecina River on 1 July. There, the division became involved in a four-day battle to secure the fortified town of Casole d'Elsa, until relieved by the 88th Division. Concurrently with this, 36th Division had been advancing along the coast, following Route 1, until being relieved by 34th Division at Piombino on 27 June.

Three days later, the 34th Division reached the outskirts of Cecina, a town the Germans were determined to use as a strongpoint at the end of the Cecina-Reigel Line. Here, the Americans ran up against 16. SS-Panzergrenadier-Division, a unit composed of young but expertly trained troops, and 19. Luftwaffe-Feld-Division, comprising well-trained and well-armed ex-Luftwaffe personnel, but a unit that had suffered heavy losses from air attacks earlier in the month. On paper, both divisions appeared to be well supported by artillery units, though ammunition supplies for them were very low. In addition to their own Sturmgeschütz (StuG) III assault guns and Marder III tank destroyers, the SS troops could call upon some Tigers from schwere Panzer-Abteilung 504.

The attack on Cecina was launched on 29 June by 133 Regiment, 34th Division, with the 752nd Tank Battalion in support. Simultaneously with this, 135 and 168 Regiments pushed northward to the east to block any potential counter-attacks by the Germans from this direction. What followed was two days of heavy fighting as 133 Regiment fought to gain control of the town.

At 4.00 pm on 1 July, with the main part of the town secured, Company B, 752nd Tank Battalion, was ordered to move in to support

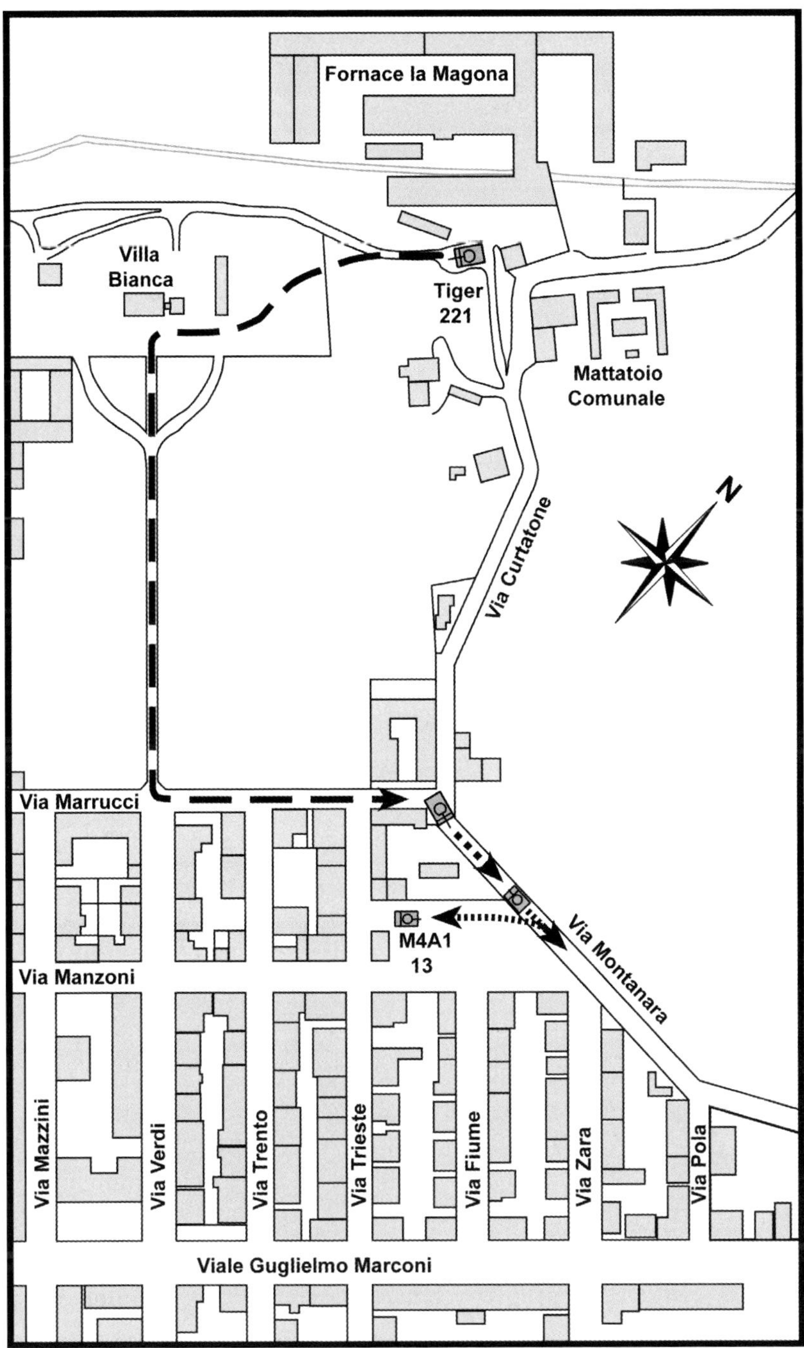

A map of Cecina showing the movement of Leutnant Wilhelm Keitel's Tiger 221 and Lieutenant Edwin Cox's Sherman.

an attack by 1st Battalion, 133 Regiment, towards the west edge of the town. Prior to departing Cecina, the Company E commander from 133 Regiment managed to convince the Company B commander from 752nd Tank Battalion to leave 3 Platoon under Lieutenant Edwin Cox in the town with some infantry. This proved to be fortuitous, because at 8.30 pm that evening, two Tigers under the command of Leutnant Wilhelm Keitel from 2. Zug (platoon), 2. Kompanie, schwere Panzer-Abteilung 504, launched a probe into the town. Accompanying Keitel's tanks was a StuG III from Panzerjäger-Abteilung 16 and around fifty grenadiers from SS-Panzergrenadier-Regiment 35, while guiding them was an SS-Panzergrenadier stationed as a spotter just beyond the junction of the Via Montanara with the Via Manzoni. With Keitel's Tiger 221 in the lead, they halted briefly behind the Fornace La Magona brick factory in the northern part of the town before swinging westwards towards the Villa Bianca. At the villa, they turned left onto a road towards the Via Marrucci and left again towards its junction with the Via Montanara.[4]

Fortunately, Cox had received a radio message at 8.30 pm that the Germans were launching a counter-attack, and he sighted them shortly afterwards as they moved out from behind the brick factory. In response, the infantry from 133 Regiment took cover in the buildings of the town, while Cox dispersed his platoon. He then set off northwestwards along the Via Montanara in his M4A1, his attention being drawn to the antics of the German spotter, who would appear momentarily every few seconds from his hiding place in a ditch. Undeterred, Cox's tank continued on just past the junction with the Via Manzoni, only to see the German stand up again, his crew responding with a burst of machine-gun fire, cutting the soldier down. US artillery fire then started to fall on the German column, causing casualties among them. The SS-Panzergrenadiers tightened their ranks in response, only to consequently suffer more casualties.

Then, just as the infantry spotter fell clutching his stomach, Cox saw the long barrel of Tiger 211 emerge from behind a two-storey house at the junction of the Via Montanara with the Via Marrucci, some 75–100 yards away, followed shortly afterwards by the whole tank. Lowering himself into the turret, Cox ordered his gunner to fire.

> 'Both tanks fired simultaneously. The Tiger's 88mm shell struck the ground close to the left side of Cox's Sherman.

> The concussion lifted the left side of the tank off the ground but caused no damage. … At the same instance the Sherman fired a 75mm armour-piercing round, hitting the lower front 100mm thick hull plate of the Tiger. The shell merely bounced off the Tiger, the only damage being a chip in its Zimmerit [anti-magnetic paste] coating. The two tanks momentarily lost sight of each other in the dust raised by their firing and movement. The Tiger crew was further handicapped by the loss of their infantry spotter. Cox ordered his driver to back up into the dust, turn left through a small garden and position the tank tightly against the wall of a two-storey house midway between Via Manzoni and Via Marrucci. … Cox then traversed the turret to the rear of his tank, putting the main gun at the 5 o'clock position.'[5]

Anticipating that the Tiger would continue along on its original route, Cox remained half out of his commander's hatch. This left his driver with a view of the Via Trieste, where he was able to watch as the commander of No. 13 tank, less than a block away on Via Trieste, repeatedly popped out of his open hatch with a submachine gun, all the while engaging some German soldiers who were trying to climb onto the other tanks.

Cox's tank held its position for several minutes, enduring some shelling around the surrounding buildings. When this ceased around 8.45 pm, Tiger 221 started moving slowly forward, all buttoned down, one round in the breech of the gun, the loader standing by with another round. Keitel, unaware of the position of the Sherman, but believing the Sherman was off to their left in some scrub, had begun to search the area for it, the hull gunner maintaining radio contact with the other Tiger. As Tiger 221 slowly emerged from behind the house, Cox ordered his gunner, Corporal Jack Leech: 'Hold on! Hold on!' He followed this up with the order to fire when the Tiger was in full view. At a range of just 25–30 yards, the first round penetrated the Tiger's right rear sponson, igniting the petrol in a fuel tank, the fire soon spreading to the rest of the engine compartment. Leech then fired another round into the Tiger's right track, severing it. At this point, Cox popped his helmet through his open hatch, gave the 'V' for 'Victory' sign and moved out.

Above and below: American soldiers inspect Leutnant Wilhelm Keitel's Tiger 221 on the Via Montanara at Cecina on 1 July 1944, two days after the battle. The chimney of the Fornace La Magona can be seen in the distance, while the shallow ditch in which the crew made their escape is just behind the tank. (NARA)

Private Lord E. Ashercraft points to the penetration in the side armour of the Tiger. This punctured the fuel tank, resulting in it catching fire. (NARA)

On 19 July 1944, after helping 133 Regiment clear Cecina, the 752nd Tank Battalion supported 34th Division in the liberation of the town of Livorno. (NARA)

With the Tiger on fire, Keitel and his crew, four of them wounded, leapt from the tank to the ditch beside the road, where they were attended to by some of the SS-Panzergrenadiers. Under fire from the other tanks from 3 Platoon, the second Tiger, the StuG III and the rest of the force

After the fighting in Tuscany was over, some tanks from the 752nd Tank Battalion were called upon to guard a vital crossroads on the road to Pisa, this photograph being taken on 17 August 1944. (NARA)

withdrew. With the collapse of this attack, 133 Regiment continued their attack in Cecina, clearing the town some twelve hours later after vicious house-to-house fighting.

If this encounter at Cecina demonstrated anything, it was that Tigers could be dealt with by Shermans. However, it required a great deal of resourcefulness by any commander willing, on behalf of the crew, to let the Tiger get close enough. Built-up areas such as Cecina were not the most ideal of places, but Cox showed quick thinking in finding a suitable hiding place. No doubt there was a certain degree of luck in that Keitel had probably loaded a high-explosive shell rather than an armour-piercing one, but Cox was also able to exploit the confusion and the dust kicked by the initial exchange to make his escape. Operating 'buttoned down' probably did not help Keitel either, most tank commanders preferring to rely on direct observation from an open cupola.

Chapter 4

ENCOUNTER AT VILLA BONAZZA

While the Allies were rampaging north of Rome, the 2nd New Zealand Division (Lieutenant General Bernard Freyberg) was enjoying some well-earned rest and recuperation around Arce in the Liri Valley. Having landed in Italy in October 1943, the division had been involved in heavy fighting around the town of Orsogna on the Adriatic coast, before being

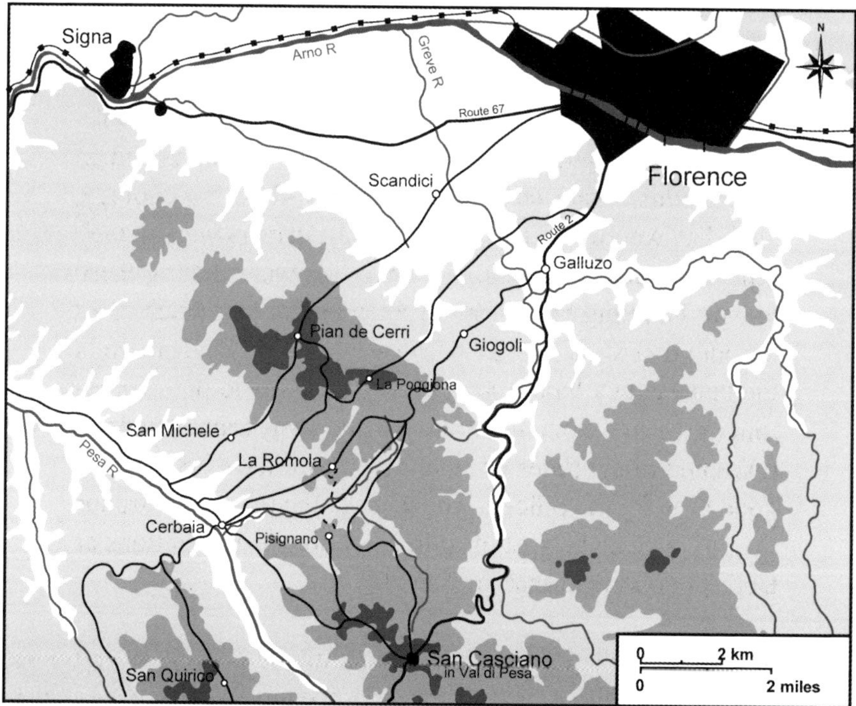

The Tuscany battlefield from San Casciano to Firenze/Florence.

transferred to the Tyrrhenian coast early in 1944. Here, they found themselves in another intense struggle for Monte Cassino and its town in February and March.

After the breakthough of the Gustav Line and the Hitler Line beyond it in May 1944, the division assembled together in the area around Arce. Though technically at rest, their lack of experience in urban warfare had become evident and shown the need to develop better cooperation between the division's infantry and its recently formed tank brigade. There was also the opportunity for the men of the division to acquaint themselves with what might lie ahead in terms of German equipment. Up until now, the only armour they had faced were PzKpfw IVs and StuG IIIs. What they saw, scattered around the Liri Valley, were examples of things to come, in particular the Nashorn, a self-propelled 88mm gun on a PzKpfw IV hull, and the Panther tank with its 75mm L/70 main armament.

There was the promise of new equipment reaching the division's 7 Anti-Tank Regiment in the form of eight M10 tank destroyers. The problem was no one had any idea how to use them tactically. The crews were left to work this out for themselves, as Second Lieutenant Ray Curry from D Troop recalled:

> 'Suddenly we took drivers and put them in to drive tanks and they took gunners and put them in to ride round in M10s, which were tanks, and they talk about psychology, well they weren't using it. Anyhow the drivers were in tank school for about a week. We knew we were getting these things. Thinking back I can't remember having much of an introduction to them at all because when we did get them in the battery they had to go to the artificers who put degrees [on] the turret. When the drivers while away trained to drive it seemed to me (later on) that that would have been a very good time for the officers who were going to take the troops over to have some sort of training course or instructions or tactics but none of that happened.'[1]

Nevertheless, with their 76mm gun, albeit mounted in an open-topped turret, this new addition to the division arsenal had the potential to deliver a much-needed lift in their anti-tank capability.

Curry had more to say about his introduction to the M10:

> 'I remember Colonel [J.M.] Mitchell called me into the office and asked; "Have you any qualms about employing these things in battle? Do you think you will be able to manage?" I said: "Well, if it is just the normal work of anti-tanking a position when it's been captured, I think we will be alright." He said: "That's all it will be." That was his understanding, that was mine [*sic*] understanding and I think Paddy Paddison had the same understanding that that was what we were going to do. When we actually got into action, of course we found it wasn't that sort of battle. They weren't going to take up fixed objectives and we weren't going up as anti-tank defence. It was too fluid and we were quite unprepared for that. We did whatever we were asked to do but later on I could realize how much we were novices in this sort of battle.'

The same could be said for the New Zealand tank crews when they encountered Tigers.

With Allied plans calling for the withdrawal of the Corps Expéditionnaire Français for Operation Dragoon, the invasion of the south of France, there was a new role ahead for the New Zealanders. This called for them to take over from the French along the line they had established 10km short of the Arno River, one that ran from San Stefano to the Elsa River and downstream to Certaldo. This took place on 21 July when 5 Brigade began to relieve 2ème Division d'Infanterie Marocaine some 8km northwest of Castellina in Chianti, 23rd Battalion exchanging places with a Moroccan battalion at San Donato in Poggio that night, while the 28th Māori Battalion took up positions over to their left.

Both units went into action the following day and made progress, despite some awkward moments for 23rd Battalion when the supporting US tank battalion refused to come forward to deal with a German self-propelled gun. Nevertheless, following the arrival of their own armour that afternoon, the battalion took their objective, the hamlet of Morrocco, while the 28th Māori Battalion ended up 3km short of the town of Tavernelle in Val di Pesa.

The advance was renewed the following morning, 23rd Battalion setting off at 4.30 am with two troops from A Squadron, 18 Armoured Regiment, in support, the town of Strada being taken some two or so hours later. Around midday, with the help of artillery, this force finally cleared a ridge to the right of Strada and began to push on towards the next of a series of ridges that lay between them and Florence. It was here that they met their first serious check. Just 400 yards further on was Villa Moris, soon to be dubbed 'The Castle' because of the crenellations of its prominent tower, the first of a series of villas for which Tuscany was known. According to reports from 18 Armoured Regiment, the advance of C Company, 23rd Battalion, ran into serious trouble:

> '[T]he enemy held all ground beyond Strada in considerable strength, including several tanks and at least one SP [self-propelled] gun. In the afternoon enemy fire increased in intensity and movement became impossible. Enemy fire included Spandau, tank and SP fire, mortar and heavy field artillery. One tank received several hits and the tank commander was seriously wounded.'[2]

> 'Corporal Don Cates's tank, hit by an anti-tank shell from somewhere round the Castle, burst into flames too suddenly for the crew to get clear – Trooper John Kingsford was killed and all the rest badly burned, Cates and Trooper "Toby" Donaldson fatally.'[3]

At 1.30 pm, infantry from 23rd Battalion were sent in to attack The Castle, covered by the rest of the tanks along the Strada ridge. The assault soon faltered under heavy fire from the defenders around the villa, and they were forced back onto Strada in disorder. As squadron commander, Major Dickinson reported afterwards:

> 'In no time our haybarn was full of wounded & my crews were risking their lives to bring them in. I shouted myself hoarse telling them to take cover & disperse … We could not do much about the shelling because it was long range & we couldn't find where it came from … It was coming from

> three directions in front & from both sides. So our move forward halted & stayed put with a disorganised infantry, no supporting arms and a few tanks holding precariously to the edge of a village.'[4]

It was at this point that Ray Curry's troop of M10 tank destroyers were called upon to assist:

> 'It was a very tense situation. I reported to the tank officer that I was to be with, who I think was Charlie Passmore. Poor old Charlie was head down in his radio talking to his tank commanders to let them know what was happening. He showed me on a map this Strada place, which he reckoned was a headquarters. Through field glasses, vehicle and motorcycle activity could be seen near the house, so it was pretty important. He said "See what you can do about it and shoot at that." I deployed the M10s so that they could edge up a slope in reverse to gain a direct sight of the house. I anticipated we would attract a considerable amount of counter-battery fire and instructed the gun sergeants to withdraw 200 metres once they had fired their task, which from memory was 10 rounds a gun. This they all did successfully and avoided the heavy return fire.'[5]

As it turned out, this particular move of 23rd Battalion had crossed the proposed line of advance of the 28th Māori Battalion, with their supporting tanks from B Squadron, 18 Armoured Regiment. After entering Tavarnelle around 7.00 am, they were ordered to swing northwards, C Company along the road with Villa Bonazza as their immediate objective. At the first crossroads out of Tavarnelle, 5 Troop was held up by mines. Then, on Route 2, C Company were forced to take cover when they came under heavy fire, taking some casualties until 8 Troop arrived and drove the Germans off with accurate fire. With this obstacle cleared, they turned west from Route 2, crashed through some trees, crossed a gully and made for the next ridge, at that stage occupied by 5 Troop. At this point, mortar fire began falling on them from the vicinity of the villa along with tank shells whistling down the

On 23 April 1944, 18 Armoured Regiment claimed their first Tiger at Villa Bonazza, its crew abandoning it across the valley in an olive grove below the Villa Moris. (Pat Gourdie)

road. Nevertheless, with supporting fire from the tanks, C Company began clearing the Germans out of nearby buildings, while the tanks shot up the villa and its grounds. As they were soon to discover, the Germans were backed up by a Tiger from 2. Kompanie, schwere Panzer-Abteilung 508,[6] which had taken up a position by a cemetery to the north of the villa.

As reported by 18 Armoured Regiment:

> 'Heavy & accurate mortar fire continued throughout the operation … Tank No. 10 (O.C. of No. 8 Troop) received direct hits by HE & AP & caught fire. Turret crew badly knocked about. 1 died of wounds, 2 wounded … Decision to withdraw tanks slightly to more covered positions made. During this, No. 3 tank was hit by HE but managed to limp

> to cover. Remained out of action thereafter. Fire started under No. 12 tank & the commander was wounded trying to put it out. At this stage, TIGER tank identified approx. 1500 yards to NE. Heavily engaged … & many direct hits scored. No. 11 tank received direct hit in return & caught fire. Entire turret crew killed.'[7]

> 'Second-Lieutenant Harry Hodge's 7 Troop, coming forward through the smoke of the burning tanks to reinforce the badly hit 5 and 8 Troops, joined battle with the Tiger, which moved from its cemetery down the gully to B Squadron's right, and was stopped in a maize field as it tried to climb the opposite hill to Route 2. It was not easy to bring the guns to bear on it – in the end only Corporal Bruce Johnstone's tank, with Trooper "Squat" Warren on the gun, was able to shoot with any chance of success, firing from the shelter of a tall clump of bushes. The other crews of 7 Troop took ammunition from their tanks to keep up Johnstone's supply.'[8]

According to Corporal Johnstone:

> 'We used H.E. shells to observe our bursts & then continued to use AP & APHE [armour-piercing high explosive] … We had to knock the tops off some very tall trees in the gully for us to see our target eventually … We could see the AP bouncing from his hide.'[9]

Curry was also called upon to assist 18 Armoured Regiment in the fight against the Tiger:

> 'The advance was being held up by a Tiger tank across a valley. The colonel of 18 Armoured Regiment came to me and asked whether I thought I could circle round to the left where I might be able to get a shot at the Tiger tank from the side. I set off with two M10s. I was in one and 2nd Lieutenant Reeves in the other. To get to where we could see

> the Tiger we had to pass through an olive orchard. The trees proved too close to go between and we had to knock down a whole line of trees and drive over them with one of the M10s. I went with this M10 and left 2nd Lieutenant Reeves with the other. While waiting for my M10 to complete its tree clearing, I went forward to where I could observe the Tiger tank. I could see it was getting a real plastering from our 5.5 inch medium guns and shell bursts were all around it, so much so that it began to retreat from its position. By the time we were ready to fire it had gone. The range would have been extreme but we might have done some good. Unknown to me at that time, our tree felling activity and no doubt the roaring of the motors had attracted German shellfire, which fell close to the other M10. I heard the shells go over but didn't think they were directed at us. A shell splinter went straight through 2/Lt Reeves' heart, killing him instantly.'[10]

Fortunately, the Tiger was now on the far side of the gully separating Villa Bonazza from The Castle, its stern exposed to the New Zealand tanks, and was unable to elevate its gun high enough to deal with them. As the afternoon wore on, the Germans began to thin out, fire slackening as they did. By the time night started to fall, the battlefield was deserted.

This event was later reported in the *NZEF* [New Zealand Expeditionary Force] *Times*:

> 'Even in death she [the Tiger] is the biggest and most lethal-looking tank any of us has ever seen. The broad tracks are broken and scarred by three armour-piercing shells. It was not these that put her out of action. The tracks are not entirely cut and the bogies are undamaged … Apart from several shells which hit and almost penetrated the armour belt, and several more which cut great gouges in the turret, there is the one which pierced two inches of steel, tore off the engine cover, and ricochetted back to damage the engine itself. This is the shell which finally made the Germans decide that it was time to leave.'[11]

The Tiger caught fire at some stage, possibly through charges set off by its crew or as the result of a lucky strike on the engine compartment by a stray shell from the New Zealand armour. (Pat Gourdie)

The wreckage on the ground suggests it suffered an internal explosion in the engine compartment. (Pat Gourdie)

There were various other opinions as to what contributed to the Tiger's demise. The account in the official history of 18 Armoured Regiment maintained that its crew abandoned it in the failing light and blew it up. Trooper Doug Bull from B Squadron, an engineer by trade, who examined the tank later, gave his opinion: 'A shell hit a weld and busted it open. This set the motors on fire and they had to bail out smartly.'[12] Major Kelly Forest-Brown stated: 'We put that tank out of action by smoke shells. Smoke shells made the crew get out.'[13]

Whatever the case, the men of 18 Armoured Regiment had claimed their first Tiger, though not without a cost both in terms of physical casualties and the long-term effect it had on those who were there, as well as other armoured units. The appearance of the Tiger was to colour them for the rest of the campaign in Italy, resulting in Tuscany acquiring the name among some of 'Tiger Country'.

Chapter 5

THE TIGER OF LA ROMOLA

On 24 July, the Māori Battalion resumed their advance northwards from Villa Bonazza, with 23rd Battalion ordered to halt and wait for 21st Battalion to come forward and take over the advance on the right. The intention was for 5 Brigade to continue the advance northwards until 25 July, by which time it was expected to have reached the Pesa River. At this point, 6 Brigade was to take over and secure a bridgehead over the river in the vicinity of Cerbaia. In the meantime, to assist 5 Brigade in their advance, Armcav, a composite force of armour, motorized infantry and divisional support troops, was to take over its right flank with a view to following up the enemy's retreat. This change over did not take place until 27 July, by which time 21st Battalion had reached the Pesa. It was at this point that the failure of the 6th South African Division, on the left, to keep pace with 5 Brigade forced Lieutenant General Freyberg to commit the 22nd Motor Battalion from 4 Armoured Brigade in a frontal attack on the town of San Casciano in Val di Pesa, the town being entered unopposed that same morning.

With San Casciano now in New Zealand hands, 4 Armoured Brigade was ordered to take over this sector and continue the advance. In front of them, along the Pian dei Cerri Hills, lay the Paula Line, the last German defensive line before the Arno River, the roads leading up to it strewn with mines and blocked by numerous demolitions. At 9.00 am on 27 July, B Squadron, 20 Armoured Regiment, set off from San Casciano, each tank carrying eight infantrymen from the 22nd Motor Battalion on their engine decks. Shortly afterwards, Second Lieutenant John Ritchie's tank in 8 Troop suffered a wireless fault and dropped out, followed soon after

The fighting in Tuscany saw the first operational use of M10 tank destroyers by 7 NZ Anti-Tank Regiment, this one photographed while passing through San Casciano in Val di Pesa. (ATL)

by Sergeant Lomas's tank, also from his troop, with a fuel blockage. The rest of the squadron came under artillery fire after reaching a U-bend in the road. No tanks were hit but there were casualties among the infantry. After searching the area on foot, under cover of the tanks, the infantry seized the nearby crossroads, 7 Troop then moving up to another set of crossroads to the northwest of San Casciano to reconnoitre routes towards Cerbaia and Cigliano.

That evening, B Squadron returned to San Casciano, where plans were set for the next stage of their advance. This involved 6 Troop and 8 Troop, under Captain Rae Familton, striking out towards the ridge-top village of Pisignano. By this stage the radio in Ritchie's tank had been repaired, but not the fuel blockage in Lomas's tank, so to bring Ritchie's troop up to strength Sergeant Jim Bell's tank from 5 Troop was added. Accompanying them were 3 Company, 22nd Motor Battalion, a platoon of engineers and a bulldozer, plus a forward observation officer from 4 Field Regiment and one from a Royal Artillery self-propelled gun unit. At 1.00 am on 28 July, this force moved off, reaching Pisignano around 4.30 am, having been forced to stop every forty-five minutes to clear mines off the track or deal with demolitions. Once at Pisignano,

Familton's tanks dispersed along the reverse side of the ridge, unloaded their surplus gear and began to prepare breakfast. It was at that point, with some men only halfway through their meal, that orders were received to push on at once. Familton later recalled:

> 'This was the whole orders from the Division and from General Alexander. We had to keep the pressure to ensure that Kesselring couldn't withdraw forces to reinforce Europe and we had to capture as many Germans as we possibly could. The strategy then being pressure, pressure, pressure and we tried to keep moving forward all the time. I put one tank down from John Ritchie's troop, well John went down, he was being covered by five other tanks.'[1]

Ritchie moved over the crest of the ridge, accompanied by a section of infantry, and moved down into the valley of the Sugana stream to recce the road at the bottom. After reaching an embankment above the road, Ritchie got out of his tank to search for a route around a demolition that would take them into La Romola, coming under sniper fire in the process. When nothing happened, he called up the rest of his troop. Trooper Bob Middleton, the spare driver of Corporal Stan Harrison's tank, was driving the tank at the time and recalled what happened next:

> 'The Troop Sergeant moved off as we started to stow away our breakfast utensils. This done we followed in his wake, up on to the ridge. On reaching the top I looked down. To say I was amazed is to but put it mildly. How on earth was I to take a tank down into the valley floor? It was a good three hundred yards to the bottom; very steep; while the track was as wide as the tank and no more and zig-zagged all the way to the bottom, each little zig – of which there seemed to be an infinite number – being at right angles to the following zag. On the valley floor and to my right I could see the other two tanks which appeared to be sitting about twenty yards apart. Off I set, and down this goat track we went. At each corner, as the track was so steep, it was

necessary for me to hold back hard on the sticks, and push out the clutch, while the spare driver changed gear. What a place to manoeuvre such a thundering big vehicle … About half-way down there was a large casa, behind which was a fair-sized back-yard. Just as I neared this place, I noticed away to my right a large demolition go skywards. My thoughts began to run riot; there was apparently more than MG posts left, and I remember thinking at the time how inviting was that back-yard, from which I could have placed the tank in a good covering fire position. As events later proved, it would have been an excellent position, as one could see the whole of the surrounding countryside and yet be hidden from view.'[2]

Very little happened after Bell's tank reached the bottom. There had been some light mortaring on the way down, which the tanks responded to with fire from their main armament. Once down by the road, they also started to take machine-gun fire from La Romola, which they responded to with fire from their co-axial and hull machine guns.

After reaching the other tanks, Harrison was ordered to examine the demolition on the road, as Middleton related:

'As I had pulled the tank up on the edge of a four feet vertical drop, it was necessary to move in between the other two tanks in order to cross. This we did, and just as we reached the position I remember saying to the spare driver, "What the Hell is the drop like in front of us?" I stopped the tank momentarily and pulled myself up out of my seat, by the expedient of hooking my elbows over the edge of the manhole, to have a look myself before proceeding any further. As I completed this operation I seemed to be surrounded by a sheet of flame. There flashed through my mind the vision of a flashlight photographer operating at a dance back home. For a couple of seconds after this my brain failed to function, and then my one overpowering thought was to get away as far as I could. I bailed out, jumped on to the road in front and down into a small depression in front of me where I lay still and flat. I was shivering. I must have lain there for a couple of minutes, while running through my mind was, "What had happened to the remainder of the crew?" Curiosity got the better of me; I raised myself ever so slightly and had a look at the tank. The whole three tanks were on fire; smoke was everywhere and dust surrounded them. Not a soul in sight. I lay there for another few seconds, scared stiff, wondering whether to make a bid for safety or whether to stay where I was in the meantime. Whether it was the fear of being alone, or what, I just cannot say, but I know that I jumped up and ran towards my tank in the direction of

During the first attack on La Romola on 28 July 1944, Corporal Stan Harrison's tank was destroyed in the Sugana Valley by an 88mm round striking its turret ring, killing him and his turret crew and setting it on fire. (Jock Montgomery)

Sergeant Jim Bell's tank, attached to 8 Troop, was hit on the hull, the round exiting through the left-hand side, setting it on fire. Bell subsequently had a leg amputated. (Jock Montgomery)

> safety. I paused beside the old tank – the radiated heat was stifling – and on again as fast as I could go.'[3]

Harrison's tank had, in fact, taken a hit on the turret ring, setting off an explosion that killed him, the gunner Trooper Austin Nichols and the radio operator Trooper Athol Garthwaite. Only Middleton and Trooper Johnny Milne, the driver, managed to escape.

The rest of the troop succumbed quickly to the fire. Bell's tank, next to Harrison's, was struck by a shell that passed through the hull and exited out of the left-hand side. As Bell later recalled:

> 'The shot punched metal on to the grenade box. There was an explosion and I knew my right foot was gone. Expecting a brew up, I ordered my crew out, struggled through the turret hatch and jumped down.'[4]

Within less than five minutes, Ritchie's entire troop had been put out of action, all three tanks catching fire.

Rae Familton recounted the incident after the war:

> 'Jimmy Bell he lost [a] leg and how was his turret crew to get out? He was in the turret, in the commander's position, so he jumped [9.5 ft] down from his turret, without a leg, got his troops out of the tank. They picked him up. He said "Leave me, get out of here." They picked him up and then the firing started, firing from both sides, and threw Jimmy into a ditch, minus his leg. Then the firing died down so I sent Jack Shacklock, from Dunedin, down in a Bren carrier to get the wounded with the Red Cross flag up. And the Germans always observed the Red Cross flag. The firing stopped. He managed to pick up all of the wounded people from the tanks. When he came up to the top I'll never forget it. I went over to see how they were doing and I said to Jimmy "How are you feeling?" and he said "Here's my compass and here's my pistol. See that the Quartermaster strikes it off."'[5]

Unbeknown to them, they had been under observation all the time by Leutnant Harder's Tiger from 2. Kompanie, schwere Panzer-Abteilung 508. Once the third Sherman joined the others, he went into action, his driver later recounting:

> 'Target acquisition, distance estimated, everyone prepared. Slowly I drove from cover. Siegfried Wiedmann, the gunner, finished them off with three armour-piercing shells.'

The survivors of the remaining crews and the wounded took shelter among the tall stalks of the cornfield they were in before making their way slowly back to a casa 200 yards further up the slope, coming under machine-gun fire as they did so. Just as they got inside the building, it was hit by a storm of mortar fire. In response, New Zealand artillery plastered La Romola with fire, but by then it was too late to get the Tiger – it had made good its escape. As for the rest of the troop:

> 'The Italians in the house gave the crews a meal and some wine, and in twos and threes at ten-minute intervals, for the route was under observation for part of the way, they headed back down a lane behind the house and returned to the rest of the squadron.'[6]

For the rest of the day, 3 Company, 22nd Motor Battalion, and Familton's remaining tanks from 6 Troop held their positions behind the Pisignano ridge. The following morning, they were relieved by C Squadron, 20 Armoured Regiment.

The next attempt to take La Romola did not take place until the end of July, as the German defenders along the Paula Line had begun to respond strongly to the New Zealand attacks. While 4 Armoured Brigade had been moving up to La Romola, 6 Brigade had managed to secure a bridgehead over the Pesa River at Cerbaia and launched a series of attacks up the ridges to the west of the one on which La Romola stood. These included the ridge leading up to San Michele a Torri and another between it and La Romola.

Starting after midnight on 28 July, a combined force of the 24th and 26th Battalions, with tank support coming from 19 Armoured Regiment, attacked up the centre ridge. During this, C Company, 26th Battalion, had reached their objective, Point 281, but they were eventually driven off it by a strong German counter-attack, two tanks being destroyed in the process, with a further four damaged. A second attack by 24th Battalion on San Michele the following night, also with 19 Armoured Regiment in support, succeeded in taking this hamlet. However, they came under a series of heavy counter-attacks throughout the rest of the day. At one stage this reduced their hold on the village to a platoon in the badly damaged church until the Germans withdrew, allowing 6 Brigade to secure San Michele.

Thus, by the end of the month, the division found itself hemmed in behind its bridgehead over the Pesa River, facing an enemy now willing to fight for every inch of ground. On the evening of 29 July, leaving 6 Brigade holding the left flank of the division, Freyberg moved 5 Brigade over to the right with the intention of making his main effort there. At the same time, 20 Armoured Regiment came under the command of 5 Brigade, less C Squadron, which was to remain with the 22nd Motor Battalion at Pisignano.

On 30 July, A Company from 23rd Battalion was ordered to attack the village of Sant'Andrea, an assault led in person by their battalion commander, Lieutenant Colonel Sandy Thomas, after some men from the company showed reluctance to go forward. Attached to them was 4 Troop, 20 Armoured Regiment, under the command of Lieutenant Logan Colmore-Williams, which set off around dawn down into the gulley in front of the village, albeit, to their chagrin, silhouetted by the light of burning haystacks. After finding a way around a blown culvert, Colmore-Williams and another tank headed off for the village with the infantry, leaving the crew of the other tank from his troop to improve their access across the gully.

Once in Sant'Andrea itself, the infantry from A Company began to clear out the village, while the tanks took up anti-tank positions and shot up snipers and machine-gun posts, until a Tiger tank, backed up by a self-propelled gun and fifty or sixty fallschirmjäger troops counter-attacked. Coming in initially from the left flank and then switching to the right, the Tiger and SP gun proceeded to shoot up the infantry, prompting Colmore-Williams to call up the tank back at the crossing. With its help, they managed to break up the counter-attack but were unable to dislodge the Tiger. Support from 7 Anti-Tank Regiment was also requested; two M10 tank destroyers were sent but were unable to get forward because of the state of the road. Then the German paratroopers, advancing through the olive trees and corn, attacked Lance Sergeant Leo Cook's tank with a grenade, wounding Colemore-Williams while he was returning on foot from helping Cook find a location for his tank. The tanks responded by raking the olive trees with their machine guns, firing into the trees with their main armament to create airbursts, eventually beating off the attack.

It was at that point that the Tiger moved up to threaten the troop:

> 'Supported by a bazooka team, the Tiger then moved down the street through the village and our infantry called for support. As Colmore-Williams moved his tank round the church into a firing position a "bazooka man" rose up and rested his bazooka against an olive tree to aim. The tank's

> gunner "gave him a 75-mm HE all to himself" and Dave Coppin, the spare driver, sprayed the area with the bow gun. The other tanks also opened fire, causing many casualties: the bazooka team was wiped out and fifteen enemy dead were afterwards counted close by. Although some very accurate mortar fire troubled the troop for some time, the enemy infantry left the tanks alone. The Tiger still had to be kept at bay. A bend in the road allowed it to come within about 100 yards of the troop commander's tank before it came into view. When it ventured round the bend it was blinded by a round or two of smoke and chased back into cover, tail first, with six or seven armour-piercing and high-explosive shells buzzing around its ears.'[7]

Colemore-Williams then withdrew his tank behind the church and placed Cook's tank (now under the command of Trooper William Greenall) in a firing position should the Tiger return. Later, his troop withdrew from the town.

With Sant'Andrea secure, the focus of the New Zealand effort swung back to La Romola, the 22nd Motor Battalion renewing its attack at 1.00 am on the morning of 31 July. This time, the Germans, alerted to the attack, opened up with artillery first, blasting the Sugana Valley below La Romola. This resulted in a reduction in visibility to almost zero in the valley by the time the New Zealand barrage began. In a matter of minutes, communications failed between battalion HQ and the companies and between company HQs and the platoons. As a result, the attack broke up into actions of small groups of men. As for the tanks, 11 Troop had to wait for several hours for a bulldozer to prepare a deviation in the road, only to be put on the wrong track by the engineers. That was the last they saw of their infantry. In the end, the troop followed the same road used by 8 Troop in its fatal attack earlier in the month. Elsewhere, the corporal's tank in 12 Troop dropped out with mechanical problems, while Sergeant Owen Hughes's became stuck after the road gave way under it.

The first to reach the town was 15 Platoon from the 22nd Battalion, after taking out two machine-gun posts and occupying a two-storied house on the edge of the village. They were joined around 3.00 am by 13 Platoon and later by 14 Platoon. Around dawn, 6 Platoon entered the eastern outskirts of La Romola, followed later by 5 Platoon. Shortly after dawn, the tanks of 9 Troop linked up with the infantry. It was then left to 5 Platoon to yield one of the most spectacular prizes of the 2nd New Zealand Division in Italy:

> 'Lieutenant Arthur Woolcott, with a small party including Lance-Sergeant Ken Stevens, Lance-Corporal Kevin Dillon, and Private "Snow" Dodunski, crossed over to the right of the road on the fringe of La Romola and began searching an inverted "V" of houses. Approaching the top house, the lieutenant and Dodunski burst in the door and raced inside, while the rest sped round the sides of the house and, said Stevens, "nearly had kittens on the spot. We ran clean into a Tiger tank. An odd olive branch (camouflage) was on the top and the long gun was sort of pointing to the ground. We stood like geese." Presently Dillon circled the monster ("its tracks were so big it seemed unfair"), and as it now appeared to be abandoned, began climbing onto it "when up comes the lid. Before I could

During the attempt to recover the Tiger from its hiding place at La Romola on 31 July 1944, the road collapsed underneath it, flipping it onto its turret. (Jock Montgomery)

> surrender, the German did, with three or four others. We were very tough once they put their hands up". The elated patrol (describing the crew as "good chaps, surprised by that night's attack, and also they'd probably had the war") escorted their captives into La Romola, each with a neatly packed blue bag similar to air travel ones. Woolcott, going through the tank, found it in perfect order, and tank men later took it away (the company's number chalked on it) towards B Echelon.'[8]

According to records from schwere Panzer-Abteilung 508, this was Unteroffizier Heberer's Tiger and crew from 3. Kompanie, though its reported capture date was given as 30 April 1944 at Galluzo.[9]

Nevertheless, the Tiger did extract its own revenge on the New Zealanders for its inauspicious capture. While it was being recovered

The Tiger was later righted by 1 NZ Armoured Troops Recovery unit. (ATL)

from its lair, the road collapsed underneath it and it rolled onto its turret. When finally back on its tracks, it was driven away, to the discomfort of those below, as Neil Bird wrote:

> 'We'd been stonked rather heavily in the night and from a distance it would sound like a large counter attack. Of course messages had flown, and at first light the Tank Recovery Unit were on their way out with their valuable prize, the Tiger. But in our B Echelon it was seen through a grey misty dawn on its way down the road towards them. Someone announced that Jerry had broken through: after that, chaos. Our so-called heroes became sprinters of almost world class, but hardly dressed for the occasion. The return to duty was not quite so heroic.'[10]

As to the Tiger itself, New Zealand never claimed it as a war trophy. Photographs show it being towed away from La Romola by two D7 tractors, its ultimate fate unknown.

Proud of its capture, the Tiger featured in a number of official New Zealand publicity photographs, among them this with some infantrymen from the 22nd Motor Battalion on it. (George Kaye)

The crew of Heberer's Tiger captured at La Romola were later photographed during their interrogation. (IWM)

Chapter 6

THE ROAD TO FLORENCE

On the night of 30 July, 3 and 4 Troops of A Squadron, 20 Armoured Regiment, continued their advance from Sant'Andrea, with infantry from C Company, 23rd Battalion, the force occupying Villa Mazzei and Palestra at the end of their sweep. In the process they flushed out two Tigers from their hiding place, both of which fired their machine guns. Some rounds struck the cupola of the squadron commander's Sherman, but did no damage. Just why they chose not to fire their main armament was unclear, though it was thought that the Tigers had run out of ammunition. For whatever the reason, the Tigers made off and did not return. But this was enough for 3 and 4 Troops and they withdrew to San Casciano that evening.

The following morning, 5 Troop from 20 Armoured Regiment, operating with the 28th Māori Battalion, encountered another Tiger at Il Pino. After an advance of only 50 yards, under mortar and artillery fire, a Tiger and self-propelled gun put in an appearance. Turning toward 5 Troop, the Tiger's first rounds hit the corporal's tank and set it on fire, forcing the rest of the troop to pull back over the crest of the ridge they were on. At this point, Lieutenant Mervyn Cross took charge of the situation:

> 'Cross laid some smoke in front of the corporal's tank and "hopped over to have a dekko". He could see where the Tiger was lying, "beautifully camouflaged", and brought his own tank round the side of the slope behind the knocked-out tank. Below the crest he lined up the turret on the Tiger's hideout and then moved quickly over the top into a firing

position. The gunner immediately spotted his target and loosed off two rounds of American smoke, followed by five or six armour-piercing shells. Caught by surprise, the Tiger withdrew hurriedly, "much to our relief. Our last view was of an A.P. ricocheting off his turret so we felt we had at least given him a jar."'[1]

Close to 8.00 am on 1 August, 1 and 2 Troops from 20 Armoured Regiment joined up with the 28th Māori Battalion in their advance towards La Poggiona:

> '[S]hells from a heavy gun landed close by and a Tiger tank, with enemy infantry in position near it, was reported. By twenty to nine half a mile had been covered and an anti-tank gun dealt with. Half an hour later the Tiger and its infantry were reported to be withdrawing, hurried on by our artillery.'[2]

The Māori infantry and tanks pushed on but soon found demolitions and trees blocking the road. A way was found around the demolition and the force pushed onto the objective, a line from Poggio delle Monache to the ridge of La Poggiona. Around noon, they came upon a Tiger further up the road but, with the Māoris too close to it, they could not call down a 'stonk'. Luck, however, was on the side of Lieutenant Bill French, commander of 2 Troop, and his crew, as he later recalled:

> 'We were working with a company of the Māori Battalion. We went round this corner and got hit in the track. We climbed out of the tank but we found it was still mobile and got back in and backed off.'[3]

That Tiger or another then turned its attention to Corporal George Innes's tank, as his driver, Trooper Pat Stack, recounted:

> 'There was this Tiger sitting up in the hills. French was leading of course. He got one. I think the first shot hit him in the tracks but he was still capable of moving. The

next one stopped it and French turned around and came home. He said: "There's a Tiger there." By this time we were getting well up there and they said: "No. Turn around and come home." There was a big casa there and for some reason we decided to go in there. Backed the tank right in beside this big casa. The turret was all right, but we were still sticking out a bit and a big AP hit the side of the casa, dust flying everywhere. All of a sudden it was not too good. The next one went straight over my driver's hatch. I said to George: "That was too close for comfort that was. It was just over the top of my head." He thought we were just on the intercom and said: "Put it into gear Pat and get down that strada as fast as you can bloody go." This went all through the Regiment. We got onto to the road, but we didn't have enough to turn on, so I had to back right into the middle of the road. We were just about to start on again, but I couldn't get her out of reverse. I said to George: "I can't get her out of reverse." And here was George (he was a big fellow) he came through the turret with his big paws, and just about pulled the lever off. Couldn't get her out, locked in there. So he said: "Righto, bail out." She was in the middle of the road, a sitting duck. Just before I got out of it I discovered that the gun was over the hatch. I was last out again there. I had to shift over to the co-driver's hatch. But just as I was getting out there was a big ping on the road right in front of me. It was another one of those misses. He wasn't a very good shot. He should have got us. There was this casa and we got in there. There must have been a troop of Māoris in it. They were panicking and the Jerries were getting pretty close. They were throwing hand grenades into the house. One Māori bloke went outside and he got shot. I went round to the other side of the house to see if I could get a shot at them with my pistol from another window, but it was no use. The Māoris weren't very happy there. George said he called for a "stonk". He took off straight away and went back to headquarters. They put down a "stonk". She went up just as soon as we got out.'[4]

The following day, 7 and 8 Troops from B Squadron, in support of 21 Battalion, put in an attack in the afternoon over the same ground. With them were two M10 tank destroyers from A Troop, 7 Anti-Tank Regiment. Encountering another Tiger in the vicinity of Point 243, artillery fire was called down, striking the Tiger and forcing its crew to abandon it. However, it was not seriously damaged, the crew returning shortly afterwards and driving it away.

On 3 August, 6 and 7 Troops of 20 Armoured Regiment, a scratch troop of two RHQ tanks under Sergeant Major 'Plonk' Reid and two M10 tank destroyers from A Troop, 7 Anti-Tank Regiment, joined up with two companies from 28th Māori Battalion in a push on the high features to the northeast of Giogoli. By 8.30 am, 6 Troop, under Lieutenant Bill Heptinstall, upon reaching Giogoli, received a call from their infantry, half a mile ahead, to support them in their attempt to drive the defenders off the Villa Capponi on Point 199. Reid's tanks and the M10s poured fire onto Point 199 on the German positions there. When a Tiger began to return fire, artillery fire was called down on it. As Sergeant G.D. Robson related:

> '88 AP stuff was pelting right and left so we moved very smartly and it was then I noticed that one of the M10s was "brewing up". The other bloke reversed out of sight.'[5]

According to a report from A Troop, 7 Anti-Tank Regiment:

> 'The M10s put half a dozen shells each into a stone house from which machine guns were still firing. Then, after passing through the grounds of one of the many large mansions in the region and traversing a valley of olive trees on the way to the main Florence road, A3 and A4 [designations for the M10s] were forced to draw back a little. A Tiger by a large house had fired on the Sherman tanks, which led the advance and knocked out one of them. A3 fired five shots into the building; but a shot from the Tiger caused the M10 to burst into flames, killing two gunners and wounding the No. 1 and a third gunner. The Tiger was not visible and A4 was ordered to withdraw.'[6]

The approximate location of Lieutenant Heptinstall's Sherman and the Tiger that knocked it out on the road below Villa La Sfascciata on 3 August 1944.

In the meantime, 6 Troop, upon moving forward from the villa, ran into a dense grove of olive trees, where branches damaged wireless aerials and sheared the hinge off Sergeant Gordon Johnson's turret hatch cover, causing it to fall on his hand. Back on the road, Heptinstall surprised a German with a Panzerschreck but quick work from his hull gunner disposed of this threat. Heptinstall then proceeded along the road, towards a steep cutting that ascended the ridgeline and down the other side. His first thought was to outflank the cutting via a track running up to the left, but when that failed he made a dash through the cutting to the road ahead covered by the other tanks of his troop. Corporal Graeme Innes said what happened next:

> 'We were going up the main road to Florence. I was on the paddock just off the road and Bill Heptinstall was the officer in charge of the tank on the road. I sang out to him over the air: "There's a Tiger on your left." There was about 8–10 feet of brick wall. I could see it from the top of the tank but my gunner couldn't get it. Anyhow, I saw its gun fire. The Tiger's fire went straight into the Sherman.'[7]

The Tiger that knocked out Lieutenant Heptinstall's tank on 3 August 1944 was later found abandoned below the Villa La Sfascciata. (NAM)

Later on, the Tiger was dragged over to the side of the road, beside Heptinstall's tank. It was eventually pushed off the road to the sloping ground below. (ATL)

Heptinstall's driver, Harold Chatterton, was killed instantly, as were the rest of the crew (Troopers Frank Mathias, Clive Lane and John Kevern), who had bailed out on the side facing the Tiger and were shot up by machine-gun fire. Graeme Innes went on to describe Heptinstall's escape:

> 'Bill Heptinstall jumped out and came running down the road. The Jerries up in the olive groves behind the brick wall threw stick grenades over the wall. He tried to get back to the tank twice but they were having a go at him all the time. I got my driver to back round to a big double-storeyed house. This Tiger was behind a big brick wall but it was that high you couldn't see where he was or get at him. I couldn't do a thing about it. The next morning we went up and the Tiger that was sitting there was jammed in reverse.'[8]

One of the final encounters with Tigers occurred during the latter stages of the fighting in Tuscany, as Rae Familton remembered:

This Tiger was found abandoned on one of the roads in Tuscany. (Plowman Collection)

> 'On the road to Florence I was attached to a company from the Māori Battalion. We had to go about a mile to the next objective. I was upstairs in a casa with Kip Richmond of 4 Field [Regiment], who was observation officer, and he showed me the country. It looked pretty clear. There wasn't anything suspicious about the place. So I went down and gave orders to the Māori company to mount up on the tanks. I gave the tanks orders to start up and told them they had to turn right and go down this road about a mile. All of a sudden, Kip Richmond came rushing down and said: "Stop, for God's sake, stop." I said: "What's wrong?" He said: "There's a Tiger." I rushed upstairs with him and had a look and we could just see its gun poking out of the trees at the end of this straight road. So I went down and called up the Divisional artillery and they pasted the hell out of him. He moved off. We then moved forward a mile to our objective.'[9]

Thus ended what had been a hard fought campaign for the New Zealanders, something not helped by the presence of Tigers in the battleground. Lacking anything better in their arsenal, they learned to be resourceful. Unable to penetrate the frontal armour of the Tiger at the ranges encountered, there were two main alternatives. The first involved dissuading the Tiger to stick around, usually by the tank crew firing a few armour-piercing rounds or smoke shells at it. If this was not enough, long-range artillery, often in what was known as a 'stonk' (artillery concentration), was the next option. One consolation was that Tiger tanks were often employed singly, sometimes even without infantry support.

Chapter 7

TIGERS ON THE ADRIATIC

It took the US Fifth Army until 18 July 1944 to reach the Arno River and another five days to clear most of the enemy outposts in this sector. Though Florence fell to South African troops on 4 August, it took another six days for the Eighth Army to eliminate the last of the German opposition to the south of the Arno, east of Florence. Good progress had also been made on the Adriatic coast, II Polish Corps having secured the

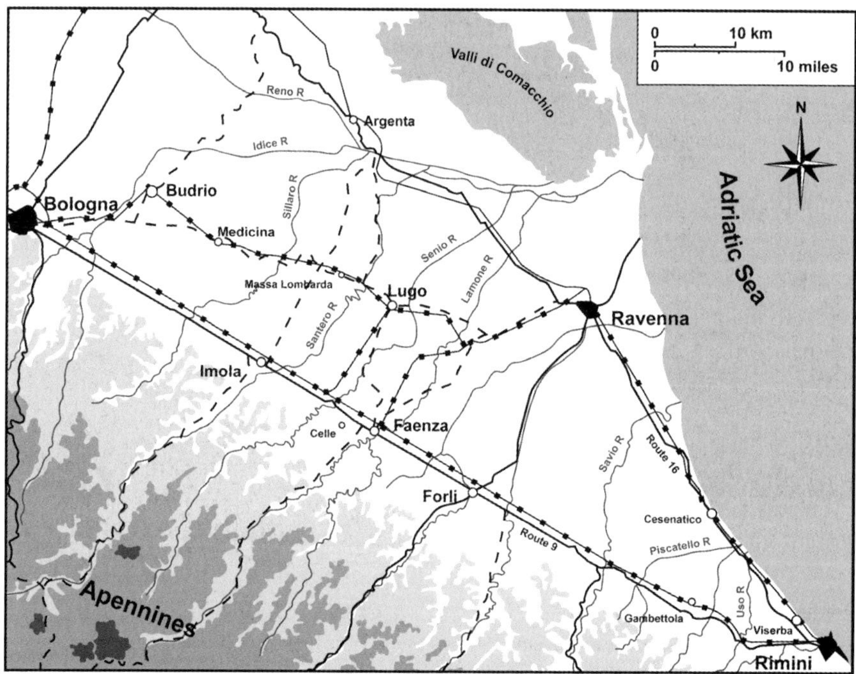

The Adriatic battlefield from Rimini to Bologna and Argenta.

port of Ancona on 18 July, a task given to them after relieving the British V Corps. With this, the Allied forces in Italy were finally in a position to tackle the Gothic Line itself. For this, the assault was to be launched first on the Adriatic coast by the Eighth Army in late August, followed by the Fifth Army in the Apennines north of the Arno two weeks later.

On the Adriatic coast, the attacking forces included the British V Corps on the left, the Canadian I Corps in the centre and the Polish II Corps on the right. The first phase of the attack called for the assault to start on 25 August, a move aimed to bring the Eighth Army up against

Though a stop-gap measure in North Africa to provide the Churchill tank with a weapon with high explosive capability, the Churchill NA75 survived for a long time in Italy. This one from the North Irish Horse was photographed near Mezzano on 21 March 1945 during a shoot on German positions. (IWM)

the Gothic Line, the attack on the line itself not starting for another five days. The ultimate aim of the offensive was to reach the Rimini Line before the rains of autumn arrived, the goal being the plains of the Romagna beyond, which were perceived to be ideal country for the deployment of armour. However, before this could be reached, the Eighth Army faced a series of ridges, cut by rivers, running down to Route 16 along the coastal strip. Although the defences of the line were far from complete, they were still quite extensive, with minefields and barbed wire entanglements covered by numerous pillboxes and tank turrets embedded in concrete. When the attack went in, the Canadians and their supporting armour from the British 21 Tank Brigade soon found themselves involved in battle against German troops dug in around hilltop villages, with good fields of fire covering the valleys below and, in particular, the main crossing points of the rivers.

Nevertheless, German tanks and other self-propelled guns did make an appearance from time to time. Sometimes, though, their crews were really only intent on getting away, as in the case of two Tigers encountered by the Canadian Governor General's Horse Guards during an attack on a hilltop village near San Giovanni on 2 September. That same day, Canadian infantry ran into another Tiger some 20 yards north of the Conca River, which, according to them,

> 'squealing and roaring, surged out of the stand of trees, its 88 belching fire … The Tiger slewed left and clanked ponderously along the roadway, its 88 swung forty-five degrees and pumping armour-piercing and high-explosive shells as it moved. The vehicle commander was half out of the hatch, directing fire.'[1]

At this point, some Shermans from the 8 Princess Louise's New Brunswick Hussars began to engage the Tiger, two of them scoring hits on the tank which ricocheted off without penetrating. The Tiger retaliated by blowing a wall out of a farmhouse which hid one of the Shermans, exposing a carrier section that had also been sheltering behind it. Fortunately for them, the Tiger took off in the direction of a small bridge, but its commander, upon seeing that its decking was shattered, realized that his tank could not cross there. At that point, the tank halted, then began to back up, loosing off more shells in the process. Then, with a last shot, it turned to the left, 'sticking its lightly armed rear high in the air', and headed off down a dirt track towards a ford in the creek.

> 'It was [the] moment that the Sherman gunners had been waiting for. In rapid succession, three shells ripped into the Tiger. It coughed like a stricken rhino, and smoke and flame wreathed the turret followed by a series of muffled explosions.'[2]

Only two men escaped from the Tiger, the commander one of them.

A more serious encounter occurred on the night of 13 September during the attack on the Coriano ridge, when fifteen Shermans from the 8 Princess Louise's New Brunswick Hussars and infantry from the Irish Regiment managed to penetrate the town of Coriano itself. Reaching the main square, they ran into a mixed force of Tigers, PzKpfw IVs and paratroopers.

The tanks allowed the Canadians to approach very close before opening up on them, while the fallschirmjäger troops fired on the Hussars' tanks with Panzerschrecks from the buildings above. After losing seven tanks, the Hussars tried to escape but found their retreat blocked by wrecked tanks. Working under heavy fire, they towed some away to make their escape, eventually pulling out of Coriano. After this, the town was subjected to heavy shellfire. The following day, another attack was launched on Coriano, the town finally being secured after vicious fighting.

The next serious encounter with Tigers occurred on 20 September after the San Fortunato ridge had been taken. On this occasion, the Princess Patricia's Canadian Light Infantry, with B Squadron, Royal Tanks, in support, were ordered to advance from their position in San Lorenzo to force a bridgehead over the Marecchia River.

The problem facing them was five Tigers located inside Monticello that artillery and air strikes had failed to destroy or drive out.[3] B Squadron later reported:

> 'Sqn moved at 1430 hrs in order & tp [troop], 2 i/c, 8 tp. the Sqn was an hour later owing to congestion and bad rds. Not enough time was allowed by CO PPCLI [Princess Patricia's

> Canadian Light Infantry] and the inf were also late. Sqn was in fire posns at MOIRE by 1615 hrs. At MOIRE the leading tks saw enemy tks and made a quick plan to take these on.'

This quick plan involved the troops of Churchill and Sherman tanks deploying turret down behind the ridge. The Shermans were then to move to hull down position, fire one round on the buildings the Tigers were hiding behind, and pull back behind the ridge. Simultaneously, the Churchills were to fire on the Tigers with armour-piercing rounds.

> 'They scored three hits but caused no damage to the tanks. The crews were deafened and stunned by the blast [after a Tiger round hit one of the Churchills]. This fire fight went on until dark with the Churchills engaging the tanks and the 75s and 95s [75mm and 95mm guns] engaging the houses and

Ironically, the Churchill IV (this one from 51 Royal Tank Regiment), though slower than the Sherman, was better in both the infantry support and anti-tank role. On 20 July 1944, when this photograph was taken, its 6-pdr gun could penetrate the frontal armour of the Tiger at 300 metres. In October, the more potent APDS ammunition would be available. (IWM)

> other targets. After discussing and rejecting various plans "C" Coy set off to [objective] NYLON by darkness. Nothing was heard until 2215 hrs when following message was received from them – "C Coy report buildings at objective held by Tiger Tanks and infantry. This opposition too great for me. Am withdrawing. There are three Tigers between the houses at 821963. There is another at 825964. Another was hit by our tanks and is now brewing up. The crew are working on one. There is an anti-tank ditch at 821960. This is 15ft deep and a tank obstacle." Just about this time L/Sgt Cox was slightly wounded and concussed and Capt Chadwick again badly shaken. The tank state now was 2 Mk V Churchills fit, 1 Mk IV Churchill fit and 3 Shermans.'[4]

The final stages of the fighting to break through to the Romagna saw the entry of the 2nd New Zealand Division to the front line. Originally intended to be part of an exploitation force, it was brought forward at the request of the Greek Brigade to assist them in the assault on Rimini. This came in the form of tank support for the Greek Brigade attack on Rimini airfield, 20 NZ Armoured Regiment taking part on 14 September and 18 NZ Armoured Regiment from 15 to 18 September. Then on 21 September, 19 NZ Armoured Regiment entered Rimini itself alongside the Greeks, before crossing the Marecchia River.

This point in the campaign marked a significant shift in terrain. The Marecchia marked the boundary between the hills on which the Gothic Line sat and the plains of the Po River. What the Allies had not realized was that it was cut by numerous rivers all confined by high stopbanks, which could turn into raging torrents when the rains arrived, while the floodplains between the rivers rapidly dissolved into quagmires. Unfortunately for the Allies, the rains of autumn arrived soon after they crossed the Marecchia.

For the continuation of the drive north, the 2nd NZ Division were assigned to the coastal sector. On 22 September, after Orsoleto had been secured by the 28th Māori Battalion, two Tigers drove into the town from the west. One remained in the middle of the main street and at 100 yards range proceeded to shoot up some of the houses held by the Māori infantry. Tank crews from A Squadron, 18 NZ Armoured Regiment, though reluctant to respond in the open, nevertheless came under attention from the Tigers as they proceeded to fire armour-piercing rounds at the houses the Shermans were sheltering behind.

Fortunately, this fire only knocked lumps of masonry off the houses. Captain Charlie Passmore, the squadron commander, put a radio call out for dive-bomber or medium artillery support, but this proved to be impractical as the Tigers were too close to all of them. At this point, Passmore went forward on foot and directed 25-pdr fire onto the nearest Tiger, but when this had no effect, he engaged one of the Tigers with his own Sherman. Though his tank scored direct hits on the nearest Tiger, they seemed to make no impression on it. An M10 tank destroyer was called up, but could not get into a good firing position without making itself a target for the Tigers. Passmore later wrote:

> 'Towards dusk the Tigers fired machine gun tracer and [set fire to] the haystacks. I then informed the Māori Coy Commander that as my tanks were illuminated by the flame[s] I would ask them to withdraw. They agreed to this so I asked for the Arty for smoke cover … The infantry withdrew under cover of smoke and tanks firing. After the infantry had taken up new positions the tanks pulled back also.'[5]

The Tigers also withdrew when the smoke came down.

On 24 September, the need to cover the open flank on the left of the division resulted in a call-up for tanks from B Squadron of 20 NZ Armoured Regiment and a company from the 26th NZ Battalion. As part of this, 5 Troop, commanded by Lieutenant Cross, took up a position at Casa Nadiani north of the Rio Pircio. The following day, the situation for Cross became a little more difficult when three tanks – among them a Tiger – were seen moving towards them to the southwest of their position, possibly with the intention of outflanking 26th NZ Battalion. The Tiger eventually pulled in beside a house behind a heavy screen of vines some 1,200 yards away. Cross called down some artillery fire on

After it was knocked out on 24 September, Lieutenant Cross's Sherman was photographed near Casa Nadiani beside a Tiger from 1. Kompanie, schwere Panzer-Abteilung 508. (Lee Archer)

this. Shortly afterwards, some tank fire was used to break up a separate attack by German infantry.

Cross's tank was parked behind a haystack, from where his crew could get a good view of the countryside over the grapevines but could see no sign of the enemy. At this point, Cross left his tank and crew to join the infantry company commander in the top storey of Casa Nadiani, but while he was away one of his crew decided to boil the billy for a cup of tea. He rotated their turret to get at their rations, but this movement appeared to have been spotted by the Tiger crew, as Cross related:

> 'I heard a "crack" and thinking the gunner had fired the Browning, hopped back to the tank. As I clambered up the crew piled out P.D.Q. [pretty damn quick] to find out where we had been hit. An 88 had gone through the turret about halfway up. No one was hurt and no apparent damage [was] done except for the hole. Within 20 seconds a second shot hit the edge of the haystack and then our hull, setting both

> the stack and tank on fire. The second shot messed up the inside so [there was] no chance of saving the tank. While the smoke was billowing up, Cab Rank [the term used for Allied fighter-bombers on call overhead to provide close air support where needed], apparently under the impression that the smoke was from our Arty to show them the locality of Tigers, came down on us and went for my other two tanks. After the leader's bombs had landed – and missed luckily – I grabbed a Very pistol and fired red signals at the others as they dived. This had the desired effect as the next two pulled out of their dives without dropping their bombs and after circling us for a few minutes, went off to the correct area, which was also smoking from Arty smoke shells, about a mile away. We were thankful.'

The Tiger was later heard to trundle off.[6]

On 28 September, to the left of the New Zealanders, the Canadian 8 Princess Louise's New Brunswick Hussars had their first encounter with a Tiger, one that proved to be a shock, no matter what they had previously heard about them. On this occasion, A Company of the Irish Regiment under Captain Pat O'Brien had crossed the Fiumicino, leaving a platoon at the river, and pushed on 100 yards north to a road junction where they set up a defensive position. Efforts were made to reinforce the company with Major Bill Armstrong's B Company, but by dawn his scouts had still not found A Company. Worse still, at 8.30 am, O'Brien's main force came under heavy shelling, followed by a strong counter-attack. Soon after, he sent a runner to B Company who informed them that A Company was 'hard pressed by enemy infantry and tanks', prompting Armstrong to send one of his platoons across the river.

In the meantime, their supporting armour from C Squadron of the Hussars, under Major Cliff McEwan, set out to find a way over the river. McEwan sent three troops forward towards the blown bridge, with Lieutenant George Pitt's troop in the centre. Their orders were to determine if it was still usable, but before reaching the bridge the troop ran into a minefield and Pitt's tank was disabled. To add to their woes, a Tiger and self-propelled gun emerged from a clump of woods behind a farmhouse on the other side of the river, as McEwan noted.

> 'Lieutenant Dave Gass and Sergeant [Warren] Rosa began to fire on them. You could see them ranging with tracers and they began to shell. They got the S.P. stopped. Stopped it cold. But the Tiger kept on coming. Kept on firing. We were firing at it with shells and even machine guns but it didn't make a difference. I could hear Gass on the radio: he'd had his suspension cleaned off. It told Rosa to get the crew out. They got out and into Rosa's tank and he took them back.
>
> 'Then No. 2 tank of four called: they had a casualty. I said, "Get back." We'd been hitting the Tiger but it didn't matter. The shells just bounced off, like peas on a wall. We'd never seen anything like that before.
>
> 'Pitt's No. 4 Troop tank had been disabled by a shell. While his crew scrambled to safety, Pitt contacted McEwan by wireless. "Cover me, Sir and I'll take a grenade and throw it into her" he offered. "Stay where you are," McEwan snapped.
>
> 'In another No. 4 Troop tank, Lance Corporal Jim McGillvray found himself in command while having also to load and fire the gun and operate the wireless because of other crew members suffering wounds. He kept punching 75-millimetre rounds into the Tiger – to no avail. "In one way, we had a grandstand seat," he added later. "Some of us could see the infantry over the river, getting up and then going down again when the shells came. And we could see them in a helpless position with the Germans around them and the Irish with their hands up surrendering."'[7]

When Armstrong's men from B Company finally reached the road junction, they found nine dead and one wounded man from A Company, the latter reporting how they had been strongly counter-attacked by infantry and tanks, and overrun. Fifty-three men from A Company of

Once into the Romagna, the advance by the Canadians devolved into a series of river crossings, such as this one on 13 October 1944. (LAC)

the Irish Regiment had been taken prisoner, while the Hussars lost four tanks in the engagement. They had also lost the bridgehead over the Fiumicino, bringing the Canadian attack to a halt.

A Sherman 17-pdr tank would have proved useful here, but none were on issue to the Hussars at this time. Indeed, it was not until the end of September that 5 Canadian Armoured Brigade received what they considered a 'handful' of these tanks, each regiment being issued with

The Canadians received a number of Archer self-propelled 17-pdr anti-tank guns, this one from 7 Anti-Tank Regiment, I Canadian Corps, photographed firing down a street in Cesena at enemy positions across the Savio River. (LAC)

sixteen.[8] Other units were less fortunate; 4 NZ Armoured Brigade received their first Sherman 17-pdr tanks in October, while in a rest area around Fabriano, each armoured regiment being issued four Sherman IC Hybrids.[9] With so few of them on issue, the regiments had little choice but to issue one to their regimental headquarters troop and one to each squadron headquarters troop. This created an issue of fuel and spares, the tank being powered by a 9-cylinder radial petrol engine, unlike the twin diesel-engined Sherman IIIs that the brigade had been equipped with since arriving in Italy the previous year. Nevertheless, this was worth it as the new tank was welcome. A further four were received by each unit in November, plus four more several days after the launch of the Senio offensive in April 1945. Some British armoured units received these and Sherman 1As with a 76mm gun, but other units did not get new armour until February 1945. In that month, 2 Lothians and Border Horse Regiment was able to re-equip three troops in each squadron with Sherman 76mm tanks and the fourth with Sherman 17-pdrs.[10]

British units started to receive more potent armour, including 17-pdr M10C tank destroyers. This one from 93 Anti-tank Regiment of the 4th Division was photographed crossing the Savio River by way of a Churchill Ark bridge on 27 September 1944. (IWM)

Chapter 8

OVER THE SENIO RIVER

Final operations for the year for the Eighth Army (now under Lieutenant General Richard McCreery) ended in December 1944 south of the Senio River in the mud that had dogged all of its units from the time they had crossed the Marecchia River in September. At this stage, plans for the British Eighth Army to cross the Senio and the US Fifth Army to drive towards Bologna were abandoned by Field Marshal Alexander, Supreme Allied Commander in the Mediterranean. Instead, he had decided 'to go on the defensive for the present and to concentrate on making a real success of our Spring Offensive'.[1]

Winter on the Senio River line brought more changes to the 2nd NZ Division. After struggling with shortages of infantry throughout the Italian campaign, Lieutenant General Freyberg had finally achieved what he had set out to do in 1940 and turned it back into an infantry division, with three infantry brigades and its own integral armoured brigade. This he achieved by converting the Divisional Cavalry Regiment, the 22nd Motor Battalion and 27th Machine Gun Battalion into infantry battalions for the newly formed 9 NZ Brigade. This meant that in the next offensive it would be possible to operate the division on a two-brigade front, keeping the third brigade in reserve, each brigade fighting with two battalions forward and one in reserve. Furthermore, one armoured regiment from 4 Armoured Brigade was assigned to each infantry brigade, with each squadron from that regiment being attached to a specific infantry battalion within their allotted brigade. This enabled training to commence with each tank squadron and its associated infantry battalion.

Plans for the Eighth Army's part of the new offensive, codenamed Operation Buckland, called for it to force a crossing of the Senio River and advance to the Santerno River in the first phase. Thereafter, it was to push into the gap between Bologna and Valli di Comacchio, before swinging northeast towards Ferrara. As part of V Corps, the role of 2nd NZ Division was to cross the Senio River southwest of the town of Cotignola and converge with the 8th Indian Division (to their right) on the town of Lugo. The New Zealand attack was to be carried out by 6 Brigade on the left and 5 Brigade on the right, with 9 Brigade in reserve. Running from left to right along the Senio River, the attacking battalions were: 24th and 25th Battalions from 6 Brigade, and the 28th Māori and 21st Battalions from 5 Brigade.

On the German side, the defence of this sector of the front had become the responsibility of 10. Armee (General Traugott Herr), with the LXXVI Panzer-Korps opposite the British V Corps. Facing the New Zealanders across the Senio River was 98. Infanterie-Division. This unit had been re-formed in Croatia from surviving elements of 387. Infanterie-Division after the original division had been destroyed in the Crimea in May 1944. For tank support they could call upon some Tigers from schwere Panzer-Abteilung 504, its 3. Kompanie having been sent forward to the area around Cotignola, while 1. Kompanie was stationed south of Lugo at Bagnara di Romagna. This left 2. Kompanie in reserve at Massa Lombarda, the unit's supply base.

Timed to start at 7.20 pm on 9 April, the actual infantry assault of Operation Buckland was preceded by a fleet of 252 Flying Fortresses and 583 Liberators that hoved into view around 1.50 pm and proceeded to carpet bomb the German positions on the other side of the river. This was followed by an artillery bombardment, supplemented by fighter-bombers, at 3.20 pm. As this drew to an end, some four hours later, the infantry closed up to the Senio, accompanied by flame-throwing tanks that began to hose the stopbanks with fire. The infantry themselves met very little resistance during the actual crossing, most of the German defenders having been thoroughly demoralized by what had come before. By 8.05 pm, most units were close to their start-lines for the next stage of the offensive, and from here they moved forward under a rolling barrage.

The objective for the 25th NZ Battalion that evening was a set of crossroads on the Barbiano–Lugo road, and their leading infantry were only 500 yards from it when the sound of tanks approaching was heard, among them Tiger 312 of Feldwebel Richard Jobst. The battalion's official history recorded what happened next:

> 'No sooner had we arrived … than we were horrified to hear the sound of a tank (or tanks as it later turned out to be) milling around up the road to the left. The Platoon immediately took cover in the drain along the road but was commanded to withdraw by Capt Leuchars. We fell back 100 yards down the road and the majority of the platoon commenced to dig in in an adjacent paddock, with the exception of Cpl (Slim) Galvin, L/Cpl (Stonk) Parker, Ptes McAvoy and Fred Wills. Fred was the PIAT [Projector Infantry Anti-Tank] mortar man and proposed to set up his mortar on the road to take a crack at the tank as it went past at a distance of 50 to 75 yards. Capt Leuchars was approached by the two corporals and while Cpl Galvin was asking permission, L/Cpl Parker picked up the PIAT from the road and with Mac and Fred took up a position on the corners of the crossroads, Mac being on the left-hand side of the road with a Tommy and Stonk and Fred on the right-hand side with the PIAT and a Tommy. After a wait of a couple of minutes the first two 88[mm] SP guns came out of the mist nose to tail followed by a Tiger tank. For a few tense moments we thought they were going to spin round the corner but to our relief they passed straight by within 3 feet of us. When the Tiger had passed us about two yards L/Cpl Parker squeezed the trigger of the PIAT but to our amazement nothing happened. He squeezed again and still nothing happened. He suddenly realized the safety catch was still applied but Pte Wills reached over and released it. By that time the tanks had disappeared in the mist so L/Cpl Parker picked up the PIAT and went charging down the road after them. As soon as he caught sight of the rear of the end tank he got down and let a shot go, which hit the Tiger and put it out of action. Pte McAvoy in the meantime decided to

> find out what was going on and ran down the road in time to see a shower of sparks as the PIAT bomb hit the tank. Neither waited to fire another shot "just to make sure" but picked up the PIAT and retreated as fast as their legs would carry them to the corner, where they picked up Pte Wills and returned to the platoon where everyone was wondering what was going on.'[2]

According to schwere Panzer-Abteilung 504 records, Jobst was shot and killed later when he rose out of the ditch to surrender.[3]

Over to their right, the 24th NZ Battalion encountered more Tigers after reaching the town of Barbiano, among them Tiger 332 of Unteroffizier Milch:

> 'When the leading troops passed through its eastern outskirts, Barbiano had appeared like a place of the dead,

New Zealand infantry make their way past the wreck of Unteroffizier Milch's Tiger 332 after their crossing of the Senio River. It was knocked out by a soldier from D Company, 24th Battalion, with a PIAT gun on the night of 9/10 April 1945. (George Kaye)

> but as D Company came through to mop up the village three Tiger tanks emerged from among its ruins. The PIAT gunners waited on either side of the road and fired into the rear of each tank as it passed. The last one showed signs of distress and was later found broken down about half a mile away.'[4]

Several other Tigers from 3. Kompanie fared a little better in their encounters with the 24th Battalion:

> 'Struggling through vines and across ditches in rear of A Company, Boord's men emerged on to the Barbiano road, along which a Tiger tank with lights on moved slowly towards them through the dense fog and darkness. Corporal Pourtney at once got his men into a ditch. Since it was impossible to see more than a few feet, the PIAT gun was of little use, but as the tank passed by Pountney noticed four Germans armed with rifles riding on the back. Springing up, he threatened them with his tommy gun, upon which they dismounted and were made prisoner, while the tank went on its way. As the company moved on to its objective east of Barbiano, three more Tiger tanks passed the crossroads and disappeared towards Lugo.'[5]

Despite the confusion that night, by the morning of 10 April the leading battalions of the New Zealand Division had reached their objectives, with 26th Battalion having moved into a position where they could protect the left flank. That morning, they set off and by mid-morning most had reached their next objective, the Canale di Lugo, the town of Lugo itself being entered by the 21st Battalion, who found that some partisans had taken control of it. Their supporting tanks met them there around midday.

More resistance was met, however, when they tried to push on beyond the almost dry canal, tanks from 18 NZ Armoured Regiment coming under 88mm fire from their right flank shortly afterwards. Attempts to bring down fire from some Sextons (self-propelled 25-pdrs) came to naught when their OP tank was knocked out, killing its commander and crew. Eventually, the target was engaged by other artillery and a tank from C Squadron. Later, a Tiger was found abandoned, its track broken by shellfire.

The advance towards the Scolo Tratturo was then taken over by the 23rd Battalion, with A Squadron in support. There they ran into opposition, which included another Tiger concealed behind a couple of houses. Syd Hemsley from 18 Armoured Regiment related what happened to his tank:

> 'We crossed over the Senio River fairly early in the morning and moved up a few miles on the other side of the Senio. We were moving across the paddocks and we made for this metal road (a farm road actually). We were just going on to this road when we saw about three Tommy tanks that had been knocked out. About a couple of hundred yards further on was an Eytie house. We could see the rest of our troop sheltering behind this house so we thought: "Christ, we'd better get going." So we went hurtling up this road and dived in behind this house. We said: "What's going on?" The [others in the troop] said: "We think there's a Tiger just further up the road. That's the one that got those Tommy tanks that you passed and we've got to clean him out somehow." This would have been in the afternoon. There were times that we used to take turns at being the front tank. Well, it was our turn to be a leading tank. So we backed up and went round the left of the house, across the paddock and across this kind of drain. We noticed the infantry were crouched down in this long drain and, the next minute, an officer came running alongside the tank. He was pointing over to his right and then he disappeared. By this time we were over the drain and we slowed down, pulled up more or less, and before we could do anything else there was one bloody great big flash and crash. It was either an 88 or a Tiger Tank. He'd seen us before we saw him and he just dropped us. He just knocked us clean out. We all got out of it luckily. I was sitting in the spare driver's seat at the time and just in front of me there was a sort of luggage

> rack where we used to keep all our odds and ends, personal things. I had just put my feet up on this rack to give them a rest and more or less at the same time as I put my feet up, this bloody 88 came belting through. We went back the next day and worked out what had happened. The 88 had come through on my side, gone under my legs, hit the gear box and smashed that to bits, whizzed round and finished up underneath the seat. According to theory, I should have been killed – or [have needed] two artificial legs where mine had been. There was just one big sheet of flame and one hell of a roar. I didn't know it at the time, but I was told by one of my cobbers, that one of the tanks behind us said they only saw four blokes get out and then after a while they saw me get out. They said I climbed out, stood in front of the tank, shook my fist in the general direction of where Jerry was and took off.'[6]

Hemsley and the survivors stayed overnight in a house nearby. Hoping to get another tank soon, he discovered that his foot was swelling, the result of some shrapnel embedded in it. As a result, he was hospitalized. When he rejoined his unit, the war in Italy was well and truly over.

All in all, it was a mixed night for the Tigers. While most got away, those that did succumb were picked off easily by infantry in the dark, when it was possible to get close to the tanks with their man-portable PIAT guns. Unlike the American bazooka, the PIAT gun was essentially based on a spigot-mortar system that had started life on an old Home Guard weapon, the Blacker Bombard. Though of shorter range than the bazooka, it had the advantage that it had no back blast, so could be fired from inside buildings. On the downside, it was heavy, had a powerful recoil and there were difficulties in cocking the weapon. Nevertheless, it gave the infantry something to use against tanks that was better than their old Boys anti-tank rifle.

Chapter 9

MASSA LOMBARDA

The next phase of the advance of the 2nd NZ Division saw the 28th Māori Battalion – with B Squadron, 18 Armoured Regiment, in support – push on towards the Santerno River, reaching it that evening. Over to their left, 6 NZ Brigade was also able to draw up to the line. Thus, the Germans had failed in their intention to delay the advance significantly at the Canale di Lugo or Scolo Tratturo. Worse still for the defenders, both battalions of 289. Infanterie-Regiment had been almost destroyed in this advance, while II. Bataillon, 290. Infanterie-Regiment, had been badly mauled, only managing to extricate its I. Bataillon from Cotignola. After holding off several attacks, 1. Komanie, schwere Panzer-Abteilung 504, withdrew across the Santerno, but not by way of the bridge near Sant'Agata sul Santerno as this had been damaged by shellfire.

Instead, they were diverted to a smaller bridge, although this was still under shellfire. One Tiger under the command of Unteroffizier Ludwig missed the bridge and plunged into the river, its driver blinded by the shell-fire. The crew escaped, though some were critically injured. This move brought the company back to Massa Lombarda, not only the base for their supplies, quartermaster, headquarters and technical services, but a German forward base, headquarters and supply centre too.

Early on the morning of 11 April, both the 24th and 25th Battalions pushed some men over the Santerno, and by 8.00 am four of their companies were well established on the far bank. Over to their right, 5 NZ Brigade had yet to cross, so at 2.00 pm, under an artillery barrage, the 28th Māori Battalion launched a two-company assault over the river and struck out for their objectives:

'It was now in the vicinity of three o'clock. Captain Ransfield reported the discovery of three tanks in the gap that had opened between 5 and 6 Brigades. The mediums were called on to engage the target, now recognised as Tigers, and in quick time shells were dropping dead on the area indicated. The flash of the huge shells bursting on a tank was clearly seen, then the other two were sighted making off in a swirl of dust. Fighter-bombers prowling around were smartly on their tails and they disappeared from view in a storm of exploding steel.'[1]

By 3.20 pm, the 28th Māori Battalion had reached its objectives and beyond it, albeit for one company only temporarily. A Company, after pushing on to a point on the railway line less than a mile from Massa Lombarda, was forced to withdraw to avoid being attacked by their own aircraft. Shortly afterwards, more Tigers appeared:

'Captain Harris, from the top window of his headquarters house, watched a Tiger nestle in alongside the wall and switch off its engine. The Māoris kept studiously out of sight; the turret top opened and one of the crew sat on the edge for a while and conversed with others in the bowels of the Tiger. Harris told one of his men to slip Hawkins grenades under the tracks as soon as the turret closed. This was done, but when shortly afterwards the unwanted visitor moved away the grenades failed to explode. Probably in the excitement of the moment they had not been primed.'[2]

Around 8.00 pm on 12 April, C Company, 23rd Battalion, crossed the Santerno, passed through the Māori Battalion and set off for Sant'Agata in a flanking move. From there, the battalion struck out for the railway embankment, where they began to dig in to await the arrival of their supporting tanks. For a while there was a lively exchange between them and some Germans nearby, which the company commander, Major Tuan Emery, tried to tidy up. What happened next would have been comical if it were not for the seriousness of the situation:

> 'No. 15 Platoon crossed the embankment in pursuit of an enemy section but ran into a much larger party of enemy. "Halt! Who goes there?", called Lieutenant Robb, somewhat to the amazement of his older soldiers. The reply was a hail of bullets which sent 15 Platoon to ground. The enemy was apparently reacting strongly to the threat offered by the establishment of the expanding Māori and 23rd bridgehead and was reinforcing with fresh troops. As the enemy fire thickened, Major Emery stood on the top of the embankment, careless of bullets and disregarding the fact that he was clearly silhouetted with the artificial moonlight behind him. Waving his walking-stick, he shouted, "Surround them, Mr. Robb! Surround them!" Catching something of the spirit of his company commander, Lieutenant Robb took up the call and shouted out, "Righto chaps! Surround them!" A few men moved out to the flanks and exchanged further shots with the enemy but, as the opposition appeared to be formidable, no very serious attempt was made to complete the encircling process. Soon after Major Emery had shouted a third time, "Surround them, Mr. Robb!" a Tiger tank nosed its way round the corner of a house and began to advance towards the 15 Platoon men. "Whose tank is that, Major Emery?" inquired Robb. The fearless major, probably by this time more hopeful than certain, replied, "One of ours, Mr. Robb! Carry on! Carry on! Surround them!" But, as the tank opened fire, and as they had already exhausted their supply of PIAT bombs, the 15 Platoon men decided that the reverse slope of the embankment was the only safe place for them and they made a dash for safety. As they approached the embankment, their intrepid commander waved his stick again, shouted, "Back, C Company! Back!" and pointed to the enemy.'[3]

As it so happened, the tanks intended to support 23rd Battalion had been held up because of issues with the construction of a low-level Bailey bridge. Started that evening by 6 Field Company in 28th Māori Battalion's sector, it was finally ready by 1.30 am on the morning of

12 April. Thus, over the next two hours, A and B Squadrons from 18 Armoured Regiment and A Squadron, 20 Armoured Regiment, made their way across the Santerno. From there, A Squadron, 18 Armoured Regiment, joined up with C Company, 23rd Battalion, at the railway embankment, followed later by an engineer on a bulldozer who began to cut a diagonal track up the embankment.

While the bulldozer was busy doing this, a Sherman from 8 Troop attempted to move beyond the embankment via an underpass, only to be knocked out by a low-calibre armour-piercing shell. Work on this approach soon stopped when it became apparent that they had company: 'On this northern side of the railway there were wide Tiger tracks all over the place, and the infantry reported a group of big tanks not far ahead.'[4] In the end, work on the approach up the embankment was abandoned when it was realized that the tanks would have been sitting ducks on top. The fact that there were 88mm shells whistling overhead at the time was a further source of discouragement.

The one success of the night for 23rd Battalion had been the capture of the town of Sant'Agata by D Company. While visiting the company at first light on 12 April, their battalion commander, Lieutenant Colonel 'Sandy' Thomas, was witness to this:

> 'A Tiger tank, one of those that had worried C and A Companies, suddenly opened fire down the street, horribly close, but a flight of fighter bombers cruising only a few hundred feet up, saw our plight and swooped into the attack, their bombs falling only some 300 yards from where we stood, and showering us with rubble. We put up smoke to which the fighter leader zoomed low over our heads, wagging his wings, and swung into the attack again.'[5]

That Tiger, or possibly another, probed forward again that morning but was driven off by a combination of artillery fire and fighter-bombers.

One Tiger hove into view at 9.00 am on 12 April when a conference was still in session at 28th Māori Battalion headquarters.

> 'A Company located a Tiger and called down a "stonk". As soon as the first shells fell the Tiger made for Massa

Lombarda at speed, but greatly to the delight of A Company, a shell landed right on the target and set it on fire.'[6]

Nevertheless, the 28th Māori Battalion continued their attack towards Massa Lombarda that afternoon with the support of B Squadron, 18 Armoured Regiment, after the latter had raced forward to join up with them in time. Fortunately for the tanks, the air force had played havoc with the Tigers:

> 'One, sitting out in the open and probably derelict, was set on fire by Sergeant McNutt's tank of 5 Troop; another camouflaged in a wooden shed, was reported by the Māoris and "brewed up" by Second-Lieutenant Keith William's tank of 6 Troop. A little way ahead near a high-walled cemetery, another Tiger or Panther tank was seen sitting on the roadway, but the afternoon was wearing on by this time, [and] it would have been hard to engage accurately, so the Shermans did nothing about it. It eventually moved away into Massa Lombarda, from where, Williams says, "it fired lots of shots at us without getting anywhere near anyone".'[7]

As the morning wore on, a gap opened up between the 23rd and 28th Māori Battalions, resulting in 26th Battalion (Colonel Fairbrother) and C Squadron, 20 Armoured Regiment, being ordered forward to fill it. Like the other squadrons of the regiment, the sabre troops of C Squadron were still equipped with Sherman IIIs, with two Sherman VC 17-pdrs tanks and two Sherman IB 105mm tanks in their squadron headquarters troop. There were a further two Sherman 17-pdr tanks of the regiment at regimental headquarters level in a special sub-troop, these under Lieutenant Jock Montgomery. Prior to moving up, Fairbrother was updated at an O Group meeting at brigade headquarters that morning, reporting back at 9.30 am to his battalion with the first set of orders for the day:

> '(1) Enemy: 26 Pz Recce Unit identified on 5 Bde bridgehead over SANTERNO River. (2) Own Tps: (a) 28 NZ Bn MR

286413 – 283409, (b) 23 Bn MR 301419 – 298430 and 297409. Intention: (3) 26 Bn will relieve 25 NZ Bn on right flank of 6 Bde sector, and adv to secure line MR 283409 – 282399. Bridgehead will be secured with 26 Bn on right and 24 Bn on left. Method: (4) A & B Coys each with one tp of tks to move immediately and deploy, right A Coy, left B Coy. (5) Route: Road 293375 – 299388 –Wyndham bridge. (6) C Coy passes to cmd 24 Bn & when relieved concentrates area MR 298378. (7) D Coy reserve coy concentrates area MR 319384. (8) Sp Coy concentrates area MF 297381. (9) Tks: (a) One Tp each with one additional 17 pdr Sherman to each of A & B Coys, (b) Two Tps to conc with Sqn HQ MR 302387, (c) two additional 17 pdr Shermans under cmd C Sqn. (10) Arty: (a) CO 6 Fd Regt at Bn HQ, (b) FOO 142 SP Gun Regt with A Coy, (c) FOO 6 Fd Regt at Bn HQ available for B Coy if called for.'[8]

Armstrong's crew and their Sherman from 9 Troop, C Squadron, 20 Armoured Regiment, from left to right: Corporal Rex Pepperell, Trooper 'Bogie' James, Corporal Shirley Hodson, Trooper Lindsay McCully and Sergeant 'Dad' Armstrong. (Shirley Hodson)

In practice, this meant that A Company of the battalion was on the right with Second Lieutenant Noel Jenkin's 9 Troop from C Squadron in support. In his troop was Sergeant Bill 'Dad' Armstrong's tank, his crew consisting of gunner Corporal Shirley Hodson, loader radio operator Corporal Rex Pepperell, driver Irwin 'Bogie' James and recent arrival Trooper Lindsay McCully the spare driver. Trailing Jenkin's troop was Corporal 'Bull' Dowrick in his Sherman VC, Sergeant Lawrie Clark's Sherman VC being assigned to the other troop on the left. Additional back-up was also available in the form of Montgomery's two Sherman 17-pdrs, no doubt prompted by the report of Tigers in the area.

In preparation for this, the tanks of C Squadron, 20 Armoured Regiment, crossed over the Santerno by way of one Churchill Ark bridging tank on top of another in 6 Brigade's sector just after dawn on 12 April, there to await the arrival of their supporting infantry. Unfortunately, with one bridge out of commission, the crossing by A Company, 26th Battalion, of the Santerno was delayed until noon, the company followed half an hour later by B Company. Finally, at 12.45 pm, Fairbrother issued fresh orders for the forthcoming attack:

> '(2) Own Tps: (a) 28 Bn on right (5 Bde sector) 26 Bn in centre, 24 Bn on left, (b) Additional Tps: F Tp 33rd A/Tk Bty under comd. Intention: (3) (a) Bde Obj road MR 276412 – 268400. Codeword GREYHOUND, (b) Bde Obj MR 262423 – 248403. Codeword RETRIEVER. Method: (4) A Coy on right with Tp of tks in support. B Coy on left with Tp of tks in support. D Coy with Tp of tks to follow B Coy and cover left flank. PHASE I: (5) Barrage opens and stands for 20 mins on SL. (6) Rate of advance 100 yds in 3 mins. (7) Barrage stands for 15 mins 300 yds beyond GREYHOUND. (8) H Hour: 1500 hrs. PHASE II: (9) Dependent on comd decision. (10) SL barrage beyond RETRIEVER.'[9]

Innocuous as these orders may have seemed, they had just put the attacking companies from 26th Battalion on course to secure 'Greyhound', a road that ran along the line of the old Massa Lombarda–Imola railway line, the Strada Comunale. As it so happened, this was the same road along which some Tigers from 2. Kompanie, schwere Panzer-Abteilung 504, were lined.

At 3.00 pm, the preliminary barrage began. When it lifted twenty minutes later, A and B Companies of 26th Battalion set off, with Armstrong's tank, from 9 Troop, operating alongside 8 Platoon of A Company on the extreme right. Just ahead lay the Santerno Morto, part of the old watercourse of the Santerno. In its stopbanks, some Germans were still ensconced, as McCully recalled:

> 'We entered these short stumpy trees and were getting fire from a Spandau on our right. I was using my lap gun but you couldn't see very well for trees. Because the branches would set the shell off and explode it quite close to the tank, Shirley refrained from using his gun but used his co-ax. The enemy troops were along the top of the bank of the old watercourse of the Santerno and they seemed to be using it as a trench. They were just peeking over the top as we were coming through the trees but eventually they came together at one point and surrendered. There were eighteen of them. Some were killed and some were wounded.
>
> 'Then we entered an olive grove along the top of the bank. It was more regimented than the previous trees we had been going into, with the olive trees in rows and, in between the rows of olive trees, there was stretched a heavy gauged wire. As our tank reached the top of this riverbank, Pepperell's periscope was ripped off by this wire. The 75mm gun of the tank had been depressed, covering the prisoners and it was still depressed when we moved into those [olive] trees, so the wire got above the gun, slid up to the top and ripped his periscope off. At this point "Dad" Armstrong ordered me to take the wire cutters (which were in the tool box behind me), stand up in the tank and cut these wires as we approached them. I removed my headphones, opened the hatch and stood up to cut the wires. I would stand up as the tank was moving forward. A wire would come towards me and I would cut it. Then

I would drop back down into my tank till we moved onto the next one and then I would pop up again, cut the next wire and so it repeated until I had about five wires cut. There was more fire coming in from the Germans, too, at this particular time but it never got me.

'When we'd got near the end of the olive grove we turned to our right and went down a sloping bank. As soon as we turned there were no more wires ahead so I dropped back down into my hatch and manned the Browning, but I failed to replace my headset. Well we moved off down this road and through this orchard country. Between the gaps in the trees, as we were coming down, we could see the enemy diving and running from place to place. They were going back but they were jumping between the trees, so I used quite a few short bursts in amongst those trees, at the enemy running between them all the way down for half to three quarters of an hour. It's not very far from there, just when we crossed an old lateral road that my Browning jammed. I was a new boy and so concentrating on the enemy that I didn't change the shell bag that was hanging below my Browning to stop the hot empty shells getting down onto the floor of the tank and getting amongst our other boxes of ammunition and things that we were carrying down there. They were put there for a purpose, but when you're firing through a periscope, using the tracers to change the direction of your gun, you don't notice these things. I threw the bag out of the side of the tank. I didn't want it any more. I must have opened the hatch to do this and then I replaced the belt, cleared the gun and away she went.'[10]

As the German infantry fell back from this position, they kept going past the Strada Comunale, leaving the Tigers of 2. Kompanie without any support. The Strada Comunale and the Via Trebeghino behind it were their only lines of escape of the Tigers as the bridges over the irrigation canal beyond would not take the weight of the tanks. Among them was Tiger 211, commanded by Unteroffizier Herbert Kaiser, its crew

Berthold Dölle and Ewald Kruska. (Berthold Dölle)

consisting of driver Ewald Kruska, radio operator Willi Kornmann, gun loader Obergefreiter Berthold Dölle and gunner Fritz Hampel. Dölle later recounted:

> 'In the morning, we again made our way to the Santerno River. Unfortunately the embankment was so high that we were unable to see what was going on behind it. I still wanted to add more camouflage to the tank, though this didn't require much since we were hidden beneath the trees. I was shot at with a machine gun from the top of the embankment. Evidently the embankment was already manned by the enemy and our infantry had gone. With the barrage of fire it was impossible for them to retreat backwards. After a while we moved several metres back behind the road. We switched positions several times, trying unsuccessfully to gain more shooting range. The whole area consisted of a fruit orchard, and in Italy the trees were already covered with leaves at this time of the year.'[11]

This left the Tiger crews of the company with no choice but to withdraw, one of the first tanks to pull out being that of Oberfeldwebel Fritz Kessel, the commander of Tiger 213:

> 'During the night we had taken up a position 2km behind our lines. At 7.30 pm the enemy announced his forthcoming attack by bringing down heavy artillery and mortar fire. Particularly difficult for our forces were the attacks with napalm by his fighter bombers, which burned out our foxholes and trenches. I left my tank to make contact with an infantry officer in order to draw his attention to our position, but the rest of the infantry company continued to withdraw. Under these circumstances we had no choice but to withdraw too. The terrain was rather difficult and covered by orchards and vineyards and therefore it was possible for enemy tanks to trickle between the tanks of our company. When we reached a side road leading to Massa Lombarda we came under fire from enemy tanks.'[12]

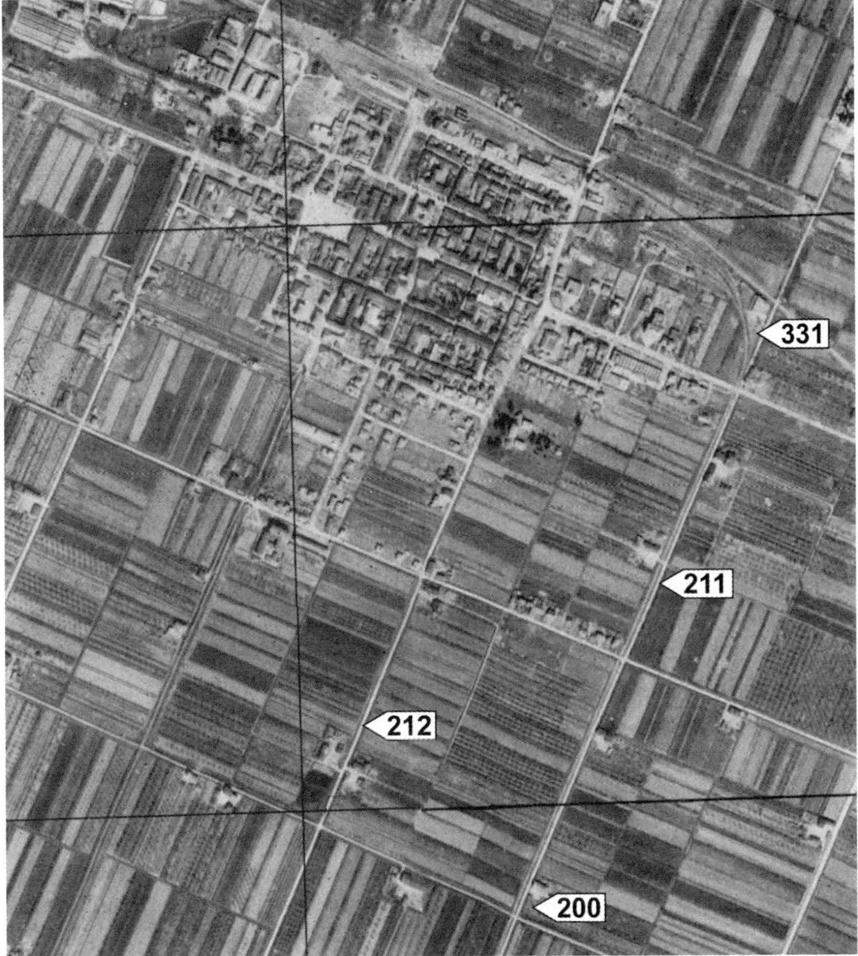

A 1945 aerial photograph of Massa Lombarda showing the location of the Tigers knocked out on 12 April 1945.

One of the next Tigers to set off along the Strada Comunale was Tiger 211, as Dölle recalled:

> 'We switched positions several times, trying unsuccessfully to gain more shooting range. The whole area consisted of a fruit orchard, the trees of which were already covered with leaves at that time of the year. Over the radio we had received the news that our command tank had transmission

problems and that no recovery vehicle could get to it that day. We were supposed to hold our position as long as possible. Although we had orders to keep the radio on at all times, our commander had us turn it off since our battery was getting weak.'[13]

The command tank Dölle was referring to was Tiger 200 of Hauptmann Herbert Heim, their company commander, though he was not with them, having been wounded two days previously. In it were Unteroffizier Paul Gammon (gunner), Obergefreiter August Rank (loader), Obergefreiter Walter Schlarpp (driver), Friedrich Huhle (radio operator) and Obergefreiter Valentin Heintz, a dispatch rider they had picked up earlier. Around 2.00 pm, with the tank's transmission having failed and being unable to get one of the unit's Bergepanthers to recover it, they clambered out of their tank and ignited the explosive charges to destroy it.[14] Having done so, they set off on foot along the road towards Massa Lombarda.

Witness to this was Private Ron Biggs from the 26th Battalion, who at that stage was moving forward behind the barrage to the left of 8 Platoon, A Company:

The command tank of 2. Kompanie, schwere Panzer-Abteilung 504, was blown up just off the Strada Comunale. (Ray McFarlane)

'We followed the barrage a bit late due to the short notice. We were then held up for a short time by a German Spandau machine gun, which was silenced by a Sherman tank, which had come up in support. We carried on without [being] further affected but by now a little distance behind the barrage. The tank moved with us a little to the left of the Platoon HQ where I was. As we approached our objective, a road running across our front, there was an explosion on the ground just in front of the tank. The tank went into reverse firing at a large farm house which was on the road a little to the left. We moved on and as we closed in to the road a Tiger tank followed by a group of Germans on foot passed along the road and going towards our right. One or two of the platoon fired at the foot soldiers but with no result as they were running fairly quickly and our view was obscured by some scrubby trees lining the road. I radioed a message to 8 Platoon telling them that a Tiger tank was heading their way. We moved on to the road and looking to the right I saw the Tiger some distance off and moving away.'[15]

Shortly after this, Kessel in Tiger 213 reached the stricken Tiger 200:

'About 1km from the main road between Massa Lombarda and Lugo I saw, on the right hand side of the road, the motionless tank of our company commander (Tiger 200), but none of the crew. Some 100 metres further on I came upon two men from it, Obergefreiter Gammon and Gefreiter Schlarp. We took them with us inside the turret as well as a forward artillery observer with his wireless equipment who we came across a little later.'[16]

The rest of the crew was picked up and taken on board Kaiser's Tiger 211, according to Dölle:

'Suddenly, everything happened at once. After the barrage of fire, which not even the smallest mouse could get through, we were informed by the driver and radio operator about enemy infantry in front of us, and finally, that enemy armored vehicles had moved down the road. Using MGs and hand grenades, and guided by directions from driver and radio operator, we kept the infantry away from us. (Obviously, our commander's view was severely obstructed by the leaves of the fruit trees). Suddenly we heard: "There are three of our people." Those three were Heintz, Rank, and Huhle from the 200. We immediately took them into our tank, where they informed us about our new situation. We decided to drive onto the road to gain more room behind us. Unfortunately, we had to pass between English armored vehicles to get to the crossing, where Ofw. Kessel had picked up the other two men around the same time we took in Heintz, Rank, and Huhle.'[17]

Friedrich Huhle. (Friedrich Huhle)

Friedrich Huhle noted this in his account:

> 'Rank, Heintz, and Huhle sneak past the British tanks and infantry and reach vehicle 211. We manage to embark without getting noticed. Tiger 211, which now has a crew of 8, immediately continues toward Massa Lombarda while still firing high explosive shells at enemy infantry.'[18]

By this stage, Armstrong's tank had finally cleared the trees around the Santerno Morto and broken through to more open country. Lindsay McCully's account continued:

> 'By this time I had my head out of the hatch because, as we got into this open country, things sort of cleared up. We were then approaching this old, slightly-raised cart track and as we got to that track, we turned alongside it. Now I didn't have any earphones on so I didn't know what the story was and thought to myself: "I wonder why don't they get up on that cart track?" because it was quite level going. (After the war, while visiting "Dad", I asked him why we didn't go down the track on the good going. He said: "Because I told 'Bogie' not to go down the cart track for fear of mines.") However we continued on along the side of the track and, about 200 yards before we got to "Greyhound" (I still didn't hear this) "Dad" yelled out to the gunner: "Traverse left. There's a Tiger." The Tiger was coming along a road from the left and, as he got past a line of trees, he slowed down. He must have spotted us up the track. I think he traversed his gun round, then stopped and fired an 88 at us. But this shell went right past the front of me and "Bogie", hit the side of this cart track and exploded. The Tiger only fired the one shot. When I looked up at him, his gun was being run towards the front again and he was starting to pick up speed till he disappeared behind a row of trees out of my sight. Next we made for a two-storeyed house which was in front of us and we knew that this was our objective for the day, "Greyhound". So we speeded up and hit the ditches

on each side of the road with tremendous speed, throwing us around the tank like nothing on earth. We got across and I have often thought that if we hadn't got across, if we'd got jammed there, the next tank to come along would have certainly blown us to bits. We pulled up in front of the house because the enemy were still ahead of us, closer to Massa Lombarda. Our infantry caught up with us and they shot in round behind our tank.'[19]

Shirley Hodson also noted this in an account he wrote while in Egypt after the war:

> 'Crashed way through trees (fairly tall broad leaves) – paused on edge of Greyhound the final objective. ["Dad" Armstrong said to "Bogie" James:] "I don't like crossing this open bloody road. We'll have to make a bolt for it. Give her the work[s] Bogie." Two heavy bumps as crossed both ditches on both side of road. If we'd stayed on road would have been for it. Crashed through hedge with infantry behind and made for cart track leading to two storey casa. Shot house straight ahead up. Two or three HEs through windows.'[20]

As it happened, Armstrong was right to be concerned in his order to James to speed up while crossing the road, as his tank had not gone unnoticed by Kessel in Tiger 213:

> 'So overloaded we rolled in the direction of Massa Lombarda when suddenly in a distance of about 400 metres behind us an enemy tank moved on the same road. It was impossible to turn the turret because of our five men crew and the three comrades additional, so we rolled as fast as possible forward. After arriving [at] the main street we turned left in the direction [of] Massa Lombarda–Medicina whilst the enemy tank turned in the opposite direction. Enemy forces were already in Massa Lombarda, nevertheless we reached the way out unhindered. Half way to Medicina we

were attacked by a squad of enemy aircraft with bombs and machine guns. But we survived this incident and searched for shelter which we found in a half open stable building where we at first rested, later on seeking a link up with our own forces.'[21]

Armstrong had obviously seen Kessel's Tiger passing in front of them along 'Greyhound', but now a new threat had become evident, as Hodson related:

'While I was shooting up house Dad yelled "God Almighty traverse right, there's a Tiger." I didn't see it. But Bogie said he fired a shot and fucked off. He was nearly 100 yards away. Bogie saw flash. The thud of 88 AP landing shook ground. Morale bloody low. Pulled in behind house to recover from fright. Gun pointing back to Greyhound again. Infantry joined up. Bit disappointed we hadn't got this fucking Tiger. Only been there a few minutes. Infantry shouting remarks to Dad. Suddenly through periscope and through 38. Another Tiger coming down road. Owing to trees couldn't see him until about 75 yards away. Wopped her onto power traverse (used to save seconds by using knee on change switch). Engine running. Bogie put her into gear and speeded her up. Things got a bit confused. My chief thought was knock his gun or blind the gunner. Knew bloody well our gun wouldn't penetrate. Pep's periscope smashed by Spandau bullet and no time to replace it. He was blind.'[22]

It was at this point that Sergeant Bruce Grainger and Corporal Bill Campbell grabbed their PIAT gun and ammunition from the engine deck of Armstrong's tank. Grainger remembered:

'I told Bill to take the PIAT gun, because he hadn't had any tuition on PIATs. I took the ammunition. The bomb had to be primed with a little cartridge that went into the fins of the bomb. I primed that as we ran over to this little ditch, just about a foot deep. We waited for the tank and amazingly

Abandoned in a ditch, Tiger 211 became something of a tourist attraction for New Zealand soldiers after the fighting had moved on. (John Nicholson)

> they didn't see us. When it came to us Bill fired the first shot and it stopped. Anyway then I took the gun and I fired a shot at the tracks because the crew had jumped out and they'd hopped under the tank. I fired a shot in case they'd thought of retaliating.'[23]

Simultaneously with this, Armstrong's tank opened fire on the Tiger, as related by Shirley Hodson in his account:

> 'Late afternoon. Light was good. Tiger completely shut down. First shot Yank smoke burst in sheet of flame no smoke when he was flat out about 17 mph. Next shot aimed down at driver's hatch and struck driver piece of shrap. Tiger stopped. Next AP hit sleeve of gun and gouged a piece of it. Tracer whizzed at a tangent. I was watching bloody gun. It only had to traverse about two feet and he had us. Don't know how many. Emptied the ring before first bailed out. Driver bailed out first. Saw Huns bailing

out back hatch and jumping out top cupola hatch. Got stuck into them with HE from floor. Three Huns who bailed out nearside collected all shrap of a hell of a mess. "Give [it] to him Shirl," Dad roaring mad. "One of the bastards is under tank. Had to traverse left a bit to give it to him. Fired a few more rounds. No sign of movement." Pep abusing hell out of spare driver.'[24]

In the end, Hodson emptied his entire ammunition ring rack of fifteeen rounds, six of them American smoke shells, two AP, and seven APHE, before the first of the German crew had bailed out.[25]

This sudden rain of fire came as a shock to those inside the Tiger, as Berthold Dölle recalled:

'During the drive, we used all available weapons to fight off the infantry. Suddenly we heard: "Tank to the left", and "Another tank to the right"! Then the rain of fire came down on us. With a sudden jolt we came to a halt and were ordered to disembark. Commander Kaiser and gunner Hampel were already outside before I had my hatch open. The two of them had been able to escape through a blind spot by our vehicle.'[26]

Despite the realization that his machine gun would not penetrate the front armour of the Tiger, Lindsay McCully fired on it anyway:

'Anyway, the next one was an APHE. The APHE hit his periscope and ricocheted down into his transmission, which virtually stopped the tank. When he was covered in this white smoke, Shirley really got into him with his 75 millimetre, and he fired everything that he had in his gun rack. When at last the hatches went up: the top hatch, the dome hatch flew open and the back hatch and they were jumping out of there. Now I trained my Browning on there [on the front of the tank] and then I switched to there [the back of the tank], then I'd go back to there [to the front] and switch to there [to the rear]. While I was doing this switching one way to the other out jumped the spare driver/radio operator and he ran over to the other side of the ditch and crouched down and ran along the ditch. By the time I got round I had a tracer chasing him and I got right up to the back of his shoulders when my traverse on the Browning hit the end of the traverse, it couldn't go any further. But I believe later that the infantry, who was all round us, got into him and they still missed him and he got clean away, so the record goes. Alright, at this point, some of them were crawling underneath the tank and I was giving them a burst at the front and back of the tank and in there. Shirley also fired another shell at them and the next thing I remember I got a kick in the back from I don't know who but I think it was "Dad" Armstrong. I looked back up at him and he was pointing to me ears like this in a very angry manner. (Armstrong slapped both his own ears to indicate that I didn't have earphones on.) So I realised then, after all that way, I'd come down without any earphones on. I very smartly slammed them on and "Dad" said "For God's sake get these shells back up into the main gun." So very smartly I shot around because all the shells were down on my level in the engine room, as we called it, down below the turret. I was pulling these shells out and passing them through and then I yelled out what shells they were. They were all in row so I hooked them out. Kept Shirley happy anyway because it filled his ring up again and he got going.'[27]

Some of those in the Tiger took shelter under the tank, among them Friedrich Huhle, who recalled:

'Kaiser and Hampel manage to break through. Dölle and Hank are immediately taken prisoner and are onlookers as Kruska, Heintz, Kornmann and Huhle are shot with Tommy-Guns just a few meters away. Kruska dies while lying underneath the tank: Kornmann suffers a shot through the lung. I can't tell what happened to Heintz at the time, since I myself am severely injured (bullet through the chest, stomach and upper arm); I am, however, staying conscious.'

It was at this point, with the firing ceasing, that the infantry took over. Lindsay McCully went on to say:

'The rest of the German crew had all bailed. Three or four of them came out with their hands up and came over towards our tank, the other ones were wounded underneath the tank. Now as they came towards us, they went out of my vision again, because they came around the left hand side of our tank, whereas I'm on the right hand side. They actually walked there with their hands up and then I lost the vision through my periscope and I certainly wasn't opening the hatch after all this, I never thought of opening the hatch. I wouldn't have either because there was still stuff flying around. So that was the last I seen of these people but I knew there were some Germans wounded in under here because they were lying down and under the tank. Some of them were kicking their feet.'[28]

Unable to escape, Berthold Dölle was rounded up by the New Zealand infantry:

'I jumped into the roadside ditch and crawled backwards. After about 30 meters I raised my head to check out my situation, and came under fire. Then, when I heard the sound of a Maschinenpistole [Tommy Gun] behind me, I turned and watched as one of my comrades [Kruska] was shot underneath the Tiger. I had no weapon and saw no opportunity to get across the road without being seen, so when Gustl Rank was ordered to raise his hands, I also surrendered. I saw two of our men lying face down next to the armored vehicle and assumed them to be dead. When I wanted to get a closer look, I got kicked from behind. Rank immediately was stripped of his belongings, and I also was relieved of my possessions, which solely consisted of the contents of my pants pockets. Even my handkerchief was taken from me.'[29]

By this stage, with Armstrong having descended from the tank, Shirley Hodson had taken over the commander's station and had a clear view of events below as they unfolded:

'Infantry rushed up to far side of tank. Three men lying in ditch (two grenadiers). They chucked it in and came towards us under own steam with hands up and stood in front of the tank. Third was the officer. Pulled [his] Luger out and emptied mag at 10 yards at infantry sergeant, who was mucking about with his bloody mag. Marched lieutenant round front of our tank. All infantry section and "Dad" out of tank standing in a group round him. Hun lieutenant had a swing at infantry sergeant with fist. Sergeant gave him burst in guts with Tommy [gun] and [he] collapsed kicking on ground. Infantry officer went up and put a couple of rounds through his head in front of Hun prisoners. Seemed to display no emotion. I pulled my pistol out.'[30]

Bruce Grainger with the infantry saw it a little differently:

'He attempted to shoot Fred Pratt but he missed, but he emptied his revolver, his Luger I suppose. But he didn't shoot him anyway. And him and his four or five others were captured and were brought to where our platoon was and when our platoon commander was told about this officer trying to shoot Fred he just [went] up with his Tommy gun and shot him in the stomach. We got him taken away, the RAP fellows but I don't think he'd survive.'[31]

Berthold Dölle, among those prisoners beside Armstrong's tank, viewed this development with some concern:

'We were then taken to a house and lined up against the wall. There were now three of us, including a German infantryman.

Just before reaching the house, we had witnessed how the infantryman's critically injured comrade was shot to death. I believe we owe our lives to an English Panzer commander [Armstrong], who seemed to be reasoning with the New Zealanders.'[32]

Over on their right flank, another Tiger under the command of Leutnant Hans-Heinrich von der Gabelentz, a platoon commander in 3. Kompanie, ran into problems. This was around the time that the 28th Māori Battalion was in the process of getting ready for their attack:

While escaping through this fruit factory beside the main Lugo–Massa Lombarda railway, line Leutnant Hans-Heinrich von der Gabelentz's Tiger 331 suffered a hit on its right track from artillery fire and was abandoned. (John Nicholson)

> 'A Company had to call for smoke and had hardly settled into houses when a tank behind the railway embankment pounded the buildings and destroyed its anti-tank gun; another "stonk" was called down and the Tiger backed out and retired.'[33]

Nevertheless, von der Gabelentz also had to deal first with friendly fire:

> 'At Massa Lombarda within a couple of hours my command Tiger was knocked out twice. First by mistake by a German soldier with a Panzerfaust, who thought my Tiger was an enemy. Thank God! Fortunately only the engine [was] hit, but I got a terrible fright. There was a lot of smoke and no more to see. Then I changed into another Tiger in position on a road of that town's exit (probably in the east) and was ordered to defend from the town there. My Tiger was showered with heavy shell fire, at the same time strafed by fighter bombers and attacked [with] bombs. Thank God they failed! While the enemy had already invaded the town – that message had been received by wireless when I was in my first Tiger, which had been towed off – I retreated. I tried to cross a railway embankment after the left track had got hit from artillery fire and [the tank had] rolled off it. At the same time I saw on the left one Tiger of 2. Kompanie with one or two prisoners [around it]. I tried to turn the turret, which did not work because my Tiger lay on a small slope. One enemy tank shot at my Tiger from a distance of 200 or 300 metres, but missed. The disintegrated track behind my Tiger [looked] like a long worm. We had to leave our Tiger and bail out.'[34]

With Tiger 211 and its crew now taken care of, the infantry of 8 Platoon found time for other matters, as Shirley Hodson explained:

> 'Infantry loot tank. Got Lugers, camera, Lira, photos, etc. Much to chagrin of Sherman crew. Another scare. Infantry yell: "Another Tiger." This proved a Sherman crossing the

road further down to right. Dad and infantry officer had conference an Islands chap. Decided to stop on Greyhound. Pulled back to other side of road. Still nervous that the other Tiger would come back to look for its cobber. Rang up for Bull Dowrick and his [Sherman] 17-pdr. Bull came along and had only been with us for a few minutes when Jack Denham called him up. Bull found Jack watching Tiger with backside pointing at him.'[35]

Above: Later in the afternoon of 13 April 1945, C Squadron ran up against a Panther. Lance Sergeant 'Bull' Dowrick's Sherman 17-pdr was hit twice by a Panther, the second round killing its driver and jamming the mantlet in the turret. As a result, the tank began to swing round in circles, its crew jumping off while it was still moving. (Shirley Hodson)

Right: Lance Sergeant 'Bull' Dowrick. (Aidan Dowrick)

This particular Tiger was number 212, under the command of Leutnant Karl-Heinz Clemens. He and his crew had been trying to escape along Greyhound and must have seen the stricken hulk of Tiger 211. At this point they swung off the road onto some fields and made their way towards the Via Trebeghino. According to locals, they made at least two attempts to negotiate a ditch between the field and the road. Horst Fahn, one of Clemens's crew, later wrote:

> 'The cannon was pushed out of carriage by the drive down into a ditch or railway embankment, thus was no longer ready to fire.'[36]

Although they succeeded in crossing this ditch on their second attempt, their opportunity to escape was over. Guided by a Sergeant Rexford Cranston from 20 Armoured Regiment, Dowrick moved up to a position behind the Tiger and, at a range of 400 yards, opened fire with one of their newly issued armour-piercing discarding sabot (APDS) rounds, disabling the Tiger. They followed this up with a second APDS round

Clemens's Tiger was in no position to respond to Dowrick's tank after dropping into a ditch alongside the Via Trebeghino, where the muzzle brake struck the road surface and pushed its 88mm out of the carriage. (John Nicholson)

and were rewarded by the sight of its crew bailing out. At that point they were ordered to withdraw to Greyhound, leaving the Tiger crew to their fate. Fahn went on to say:

> 'Clemens being shot in the head and heavily wounded, sagged unconscious on his seat. Gunner Fahn after lying him laterally over the case bag (at the cannon), could thereby not climb onto the commander's seat, in order to direct the driver. Fahn heaved Clemens from the turret and let him roll down onto the ground. [Clemens comes] again to consciousness, Fahn dragged him (together) with Kurt Hermann back [to their Medical unit]. [On their foot march] they met commander Herbert Kaiser and gunner Fritz Hampel from the knocked out 211. Hampel had a flesh wound, a glancing shot from a MP40 (Tommy gun) crosswise over the chest. [Together] they continued to march on foot to Medicina.'[37]

In the meantime, back at Tiger 211, things were far from quiet with 8 Platoon and Armstrong's tank, as Hodson noted in his account:

> 'Infantry began to dig in all along the road. Mortar fire heavy. Dad thought Teds [Germans were] OPing from church tower in Massa Lombarda about 700 yards away. Put five HE on delay into it. She came down with crash and hell of clatter with bells ringing as she came down. Mortaring stopped.'[38]

Lindsay McCully gave his version of this event:

> 'Things had slackened down a lot but we decided that owing to the heavy mortaring we were getting and the house was getting, and the road especially was getting, we decided we'd move back over this road and turn round to face the enemy from whichever angle the shells were coming from. Now the infantry were getting so much mortaring, heavy mortaring was going on, our support

troops then, after they'd taken the prisoners off and they'd ratted the tank for all its belongings and what have you, they then dug in along this bank here and we moved across the road, away from the shelling of this two-storeyed house and the roadway, over near the Tiger that was knocked out. We were getting so much mortar fire that "Dad" looked around and just above the tops of the trees was Massa Lombarda, which must have been half a mile away, [with] a church tower sticking up. We couldn't see the church for the trees and the shrubs but we could see the tower sticking up. So Dad Armstrong said to Shirley "I think that is being used for an OPIP or an observation post and this is why we are getting so much of the heavy mortaring." To which he said "I think you'd better put a few shots into that tower." So Shirley ripped fire and put five rounds of HE into that church tower. Dad said "That'll do now. If there's any OPIPs up that tower he'll be scampering down by now I would think." To which Shirley replied "Oh I've one more up the spout." You can't take a shell out again because you'd pull the front off it and block your own gun. So he said "Will I let that go?" Dad said "Oh yes. If you've got it up the spout let it go." Well that last one must have hit low down because the old tower shook and twisted and dust rose, and everything went over and the old tower crashed over. I found out later on it went clear through the roof of the church on the inside.'[39]

Nevertheless, Armstrong was still worried about the reappearance of one of the Tigers, according to Hodson:

'Clark arrived with his 17-pdr. He [was] subdued about whole proceedings. Rather envious that Bull had Tiger and not him. Spandau opened up. Nervous of counter attack. We had only one platoon and a 17-pdr with us. So got a stonk put down on area by telling Bill de Lautour Battle Captain. Arty recorded area as a DF target. Stonk shut Spandau up. After church tower fell a lone Spitfire dived down for a shufti gave

> a wave and left. Bit nervous he'd do us over with a Tiger sitting in the middle of the road only 50 yards away.'[40]

The tanks, however, did not withdraw immediately but remained in position along Greyhound for a little longer, according to McCully:

> 'The mortaring stopped almost immediately and we got no more mortaring. Well, not heavy mortaring, spasmodic stuff. But the light was deteriorating very quickly. So we remained here for some time with this conversation going on between Dad and headquarters about how these other ones were going. Lieutenant Jenkins and his platoon of infantry had come down here. Then of course there was the other corporal's tank, which had gone round over the top. The reports had come back that they received very little opposition. We were so close to this Tiger that we could hear a lot of moans and groaning, crying coming from the wounded laying in this ditch alongside the Tiger. Shirley was our medical man so he suggested why don't we go out and administer some morphia to these wounded Germans that were still laying in the ditch. The other ones had gone but there was either three or four there. After a few inquiries he asked me if I'd go out to assist him so I popped out the side of the tank and went round the back and down to the ditch. The mortaring had almost ceased at this time and it was dark so all I did was carry the torch for Shirley. When we got down the first one we came to was lying semi-face down, on his right side and there was a leg that come up over the back of his neck and I thought "Good God, that's his leg, he must have got a hell of a shell blast to blow his leg up through there" but there was another one laying down at the back and it may have been his leg onto the other one's shoulder because they were sort of huddled up together. Anyway I held the torch and Shirley administered the morphia and he done two and the other one I think must have been dead. Anyway we did that and went back and got into our tank. By this time it was stone dark.'[41]

Hodson wrote the following about the wounded:

> 'One Ted lying with greatcoat over in ditch shivering with cold [–] gave him one quarter grain of morphia. Looked young dark, dirty had that smell peculiar stale smell. Chloroformed struggled a lot plus half a grain. Another very badly wounded nearly dead couldn't do anything. Third shot through guts [and] left arm, left leg shattered. Other chap under tank or what was left of him. Burying Hun lieutenant. 20 years old 6th Panzergrenadiers. Fought Russian Front [and served in] occupation of France by paybook.'[42]

Back inside the tank, according to McCully:

> 'Shirley gave me a slap on the back, down in my engine room part and passed down a bottle of Grapa and said: "Here Lindsay stuff a gob full of this into you. You certainly can call yourself an old dig now after this effort." So I didn't enjoy the Grapa, it was horrible, but being a new boy on the block, after the remark of becoming an old dig I felt very, very proud. So anyway we were back in the tank after my drink of that Grapa, we settled down and were then called back to headquarters. The Salvation Army arrived there with hot cocoa. I didn't get any myself, I was inside the tank. For one reason I was too scared to get out and I had to get all the Browning empty shells out. So I started to work on that and cleaning the tank out. I pulled all the full boxes of ammunition up and put them on Bogie's side and gathered up all these shells and fired them out and I fired them out for about an hour, or over an hour perhaps. They went in and had some cocoa. So I missed out on me cocoa drink and I didn't get out of that tank that night.'[43]

The wounded Germans from the Tiger remained in the ditch for the rest of the night before being rescued, the heavily wounded Friedrich Huhle writing later:

'Will Kornman and me were left lying, one beside the other in the road ditch to the right of the tank. The following morning, as no help was coming, Willi Kornman with his last strength sought for help, that came in the form of an ambulance jeep. I heard no sign of life from Valentine Heintz, who was lying all alone in the road ditch to the left of the tank, until the following morning when he was loaded with me onto the jeep.'[44]

Nevertheless, there was still some sting in the Tigers when the attack resumed on 13 April in 23rd Battalion's sector. As A Squadron, 18 Armoured Regiment, set off with them that afternoon,

'Along a road from the right came those deadly "eighty-eights", and to cross the line of fire the Shermans would have had to expose themselves as sitting shots. Just a little way ahead the infantry was held up by another of those troublesome pockets with a few Spandaus and a light mortar or two. Booth's 2 Troop and Sergeant Alex Mowat's 1 Troop were now leading the squadron. The tanks manoeuvred carefully up behind buildings and trees to get near the Tiger; finally one Sherman bounced a 75 millimetre shell off its hide, and the Tiger unwilling to take any more, made off at high speed in a cloud of dust. A few hundred yards further on another big tank held its ground for a while, but pulled out after swapping shots with Mowat's tank, and was seen no more.'[45]

That was the last occasion that New Zealanders encountered Tigers, their line of advance taking them more in the direction of the retreat of 26. Panzer-Division. But the Tigers had left an indelible mark on them, including Lindsay McCully. The morning after the encounter with the Tiger, C Squadron set off again, 8 Troop without Second Lieutenant Noel Jenkins, as while returning from a conference he was fatally wounded by mortar fire. Thus, command of the troop fell to Armstrong. McCully recalled:

'Anyway we got down to a house, where there was some four or five German prisoners, very, very wrapped up, they were in a bit of a state. We got in behind the house, and got out of our tanks. Anyway I was standing outside and a reaction sort of set in on me and I started shaking. My legs were shaking, my hands were shaking and I don't know whether I wasn't shedding a little tear or two, not knowing what was going on. When all of a sudden from behind us the artillery opened up a stonk. I hit the ground flat. I don't know whether I burst into tears, but I was pretty near the end of my tether by this stage. So anyway, alongside me was another 20th man from C squadron who was great friend of "Bogie" James. Anyway this fellow was called Dave Wyllie. I was in a state where I was just about ready to collapse. He bent down and picked me up by the shoulder and put me back up on my feet, put his arm around me in beside the side of the house and he said "Don't worry Lin, they're our 25-pounders going out." He put his arm on my shoulder and pulled me in behind the house and he said "Now you settle down son, you had a hard day yesterday. Now listen here, settle down, you'll come right, it's just that you've got through your first action which was a pretty hefty affair." And do you know from then until the end of the war and the bonding that I got through Dave Wyllie was such that I never again got the shakes, or the shivers.'[46]

Where this engagement differs from others is that Armstrong found himself with little choice but to engage a Tiger head on, the least favourable circumstances he could have had. It was lucky for him that the overloaded Tiger was not in a position to respond, escape from the battlefield being the primary intention of its crew. Not that Armstrong knew this at the time. It was just as well, because an examination of Tiger 211 after the battle showed that it had been struck some twenty times on its front armour, with no sign of any penetration. Instead, it was claimed that a lucky shot struck the driver's periscope on his roof hatch, shrapnel from which entered the driver's compartment and damaged the transmission. Furthermore, the extensive use of smoke shells served to confuse the Tiger crew even more as to what was happening.

It is fortunate for the historical record that the engagement was well covered in the literature. At least three versions of it can be found among the New Zealand official histories of the war, two in unit histories and also within the second volume dealing with the Italian campaign. Unfortunately, the latter managed to confound the issue by expanding the incident into the loss of two Tigers, when all the evidence points to only one.[47]

There are also two German accounts of the battle, and it was from these that claims of the massacre arose, even though only one tank crewman died. Here it was possible to learn from one of the German veterans that this arose from a mistranslation of the term '*feuer*' to mean 'shooting' in the English versions of these books, when according to the German author of the account it meant 'fire'. Interestingly, the main concern of the wounded German tank crewmen was not knowing why they had been subjected to such intense fire while under the Tiger. This is something that only became clearer many years later after they had read the New Zealand accounts and came to appreciate the high level of fear Allied tank crews had towards Tigers.

The Germans were also unhappy about the rough treatment that they were subjected to afterwards by the New Zealand infantry, something that was sorted out by the tank commander, who they assumed to be 'English' because of the more humane treatment they received from him!

Chapter 10

FINAL DAYS

From here onwards, schwere Panzer-Abteilung 504 found itself constantly on the retreat, shedding Tigers as they proceeded north. Down to twenty-six Tigers on 15 April 1945, this number was soon halved as more tanks broke down and were abandoned, a situation made worse by the loss of both Bergepanthers that day. One fell into a crater, while the

This Bergepanthers was abandoned by schwere-Panzer-Abteilung 504 on 15 April 1945 after colliding with a Tiger during the retreat. Its loss compromised the Germans' ability to recover tanks during their retreat northwards. (Ben Hoban)

other collided with another tank on a night march. Despite this, there were still enough Tigers around to cause problems for the advancing Allies, in this case 6th Armoured Division. On 19 April, 2 Lothians and Border Horse, from the 6th Armoured, received orders to continue their advance out of Argenta along Route 16 to seize the bridge at San Nicolò Ferrarese and proceed on to Marrara. At 4.30 pm, B Squadron turned off Route 16, set off west along a track and crossed the Fosso ben Vignante, where they wheeled north. Though encountering fire from two tanks and four self-propelled guns, good progress was made, two of the SP guns being knocked out at 6.55 pm:

> 'A MkVI enemy tank, which had been concealed behind the house at 189700, came out of cover and opened rapid fire on the leading tanks of B Sqn, which were then in very open ground near the farm at 190696. The leading tank was knocked out and set on fire and, as the other tanks went forward to assist the first, they were also hit. Smoke was used to cover the movement of the tanks but a total of four were knocked out. Two of them caught fire. Casualties were suffered, including Lt J K Elliot, who lost a leg.'[1]

Nevertheless, there were still enough Tigers around to trouble Allied tank crews as they continued their forward drive. Lieutenant George Martin, commander of the Sherman 17-pdrs of 4 Troop, B Squadron, 2 Lothians and Border Horse, recalled another incident on 20 April when they were holding a position by a canal bank near the village of San Nicolò. It all started with a radio call from his squadron commander:

> '"Peter 4, report over", "Peter 4 over" I replied. The Squadron leader continued "I've reports of three Tiger tanks heading south along the road to your front. Take up positions to meet them, over." "Wilco" I said, "can you get the Cab-ranks over? It should help a bit out."'[2]

To the distain of Martin and his crew, at this point the commander of the Sherman 105mm tank accompanying them announced that he was withdrawing to a more suitable 'hull-down' position. Nevertheless, Martin's troop remained in place, the tanks spreading out in an effort to get good cover and a useful spread of fire. Martin's tank, having sustained damage to the traverse mechanism of his turret the previous day, aligned his turret in the direction from where he hoped the Tigers would approach. The troop then turned their tank engines off and settled down to wait. Shortly afterwards, some rocket-firing Mustangs hove briefly into view, flying at tree-top level, followed almost immediately by the sound of explosions some 2.5km away. Shortly afterwards, Quickly, their squadron commander, radioed up:

> 'Peter 4, you'll be glad to know the "Cab-racks" knocked out two Tigers and the other one turned tail and was last seen heading north, keep your eyes open though, it may return. Remain where you are for the present, we're being pulled out later to do another job. Out.'[3]

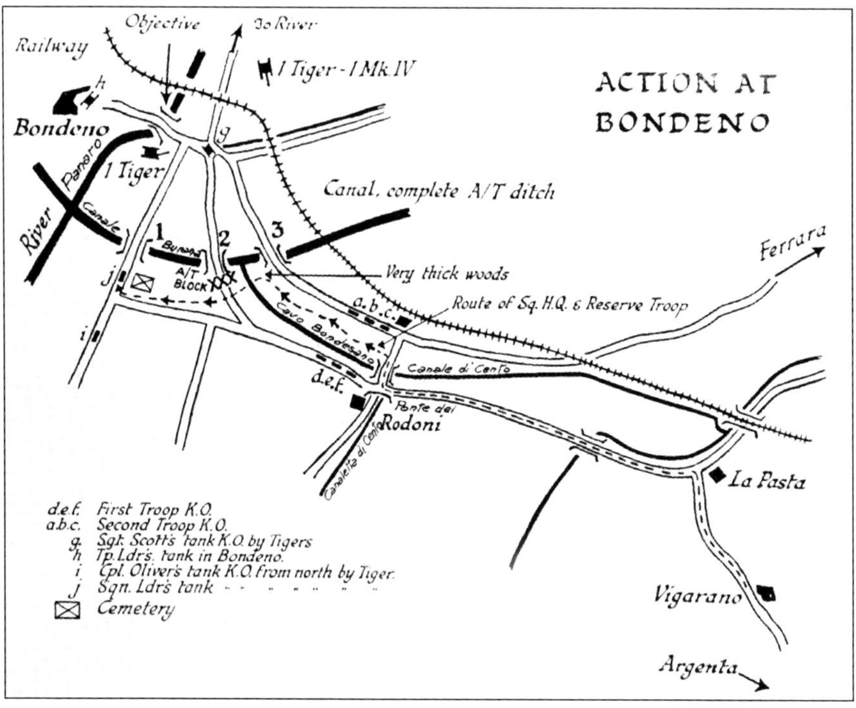

The action at Bondeno.

Around mid-afternoon, some infantry arrived and dug in, allowing Martin's troop to pull out and return to their squadron.

While this ended badly for the Tigers, the tables were turned on 22 April during the advance of 2 Lothians and Border Horse and the 2nd Battalion of the Rifle Brigade (Prince Consort's Own) toward the town of Bondeno. After a recce revealed that the vital bridge over the Parano River was still intact, a hastily organized attack was arranged with the Rifle Brigade's C Company and Captain F.M. Hepburne Scott's C Squadron. The 2 Lothians and Border Horse diary recorded events:

> 'C Coy went forward fast, but unfortunately lost wireless contact and, as the light was beginning to go, the Sqn Ldr ordered 1Tp to advance to ensure that the bridge was taken, and to support the infantry. They went straight for the bridge but, just as the Tp Ldr reached it, Sgt Scott, who was following him, was fired at by a Tiger tank behind a house to his right rear, at 30yds range. The tank was hit in the ammunition bins and blew up instantly. The driver, LCpl Stockton, and co-driver, Tpr Brooks, were killed instantly, and Sgt Scott, Tpr Heap, the operator, and LCpl Pym, the gunner, were blown out of the tank on fire. Tpr Heap died an hour later. Tpr Hunt, co-driver of the third tank, ran forward to try and help the others but, as he did so, they were machine-gunned by the Tigers and Sgt Scott and LCpl Pym were killed. Tpr Hunt was taken prisoner by some German infantry but escaped three days later.
>
> 'LSgt Richardson, commanding the third tank, was unable to fire as he could not pass the blazing tank in front, and the two Tigers, which were shielded by the houses, got away up the road. He at once reported this on the wireless to Lt Campbell in front, who had just crossed the main bridge.
>
> 'He was now alone, as the infantry had not yet arrived, but the German military policeman waved them on. They shot him with their turret Browning and raced on down the street with all guns firing, Tpr Dalziel swinging his turret with Browning and 76mm, and Tpr Morris firing his bow gun, while Tpr White, driver, opened up. They got several Germans and Tpr Southwell, the operator, joined in with

Tommy gun, while Lt Campbell fired a pistol in each hand. 200yds further on they swung left down a side street to avoid the following Tigers, and were hit by a bazooka fired from a window. They all baled out, but one of the crew was killed. Lt Campbell and two others were taken prisoner, as they had only pistols to defend themselves.

'4Tp, preceded by [illegible] canal bridge, followed by Sqn HQ. Just as they were getting into position to cross, a Tiger tank fired from behind cover just across the canal and knocked-out Cpl Oliver's tank and the rear link, wounding LCpl Cartledge, the operator. The rest of the crews were miraculously unhurt, although Capt Woodroffe had a small splinter. Alas, the 88 had passed through the two hens travelling in a box behind his turret. Although the Tiger could not be located in half-light, it was impossible for anything to cross under this fire. Just then came the report of 1Tp's action, on the wireless. As soon as the Tigers had crossed the bridge into Bondeno it was blown by the Germans, just as C Coy 2RB [Rifle Brigade] were arriving to take it over.'[4]

Reported losses by 2 Lothians and Border Horse that day were eleven tanks.

Further back, Martin and the crew of his Sherman 17-pdr heard it all:

'We listened to the destruction of "C" Squadron with sympathetic understanding of the tank commander who bitterly complained, over his radio, that his shells were just bouncing off the front of a Tiger, the sudden loud explosion and then silent radio told its own story. My wireless operator looked at me and said "I reckon they've just lost the whole Squadron sir." He had barely finished speaking when the Squadron Leader came on air to inform us that we had been ordered to take over from "C" Squadron and get to the bridge.'[5]

However, as B Squadron closed up to the bridge a loud explosion and a great column of smoke ahead signalled its destruction. Orders were accordingly then changed to cover the approach roads to the bridge against the arrival of a large German force. That night, 4 Troop with its Sherman 17-pdr tanks were sent forward, along with a Sherman 105mm tank. They took up positions in the vicinity of the cemetery at the crossroads, where there was a knocked-out Sherman 17-pdr, while in sight some 200 yards north of the crossroads was another Sherman 17-pdr slowly brewing up. They received orders at 3.30 am the following morning to stand to, when tanks were heard approaching the canal. Their report went on:

> 'At 0400hrs the sound of tracked vehs. and men talking was heard approaching and, in the light of the burning 17pr tank, the silhouette of a German tank appeared, nosing its way round the corner. It could not pass the burning tank, so the German crew commander jumped out and had a look – he shouted some orders and some more figures appeared. The enemy tank then reversed and proceeded to tow the 17pr a short distance into the side of the road to enable him to get past. This operation caused the slowly brewing tank to flare up and considerably more light was given out than before.'

With the Sherman now out of the way, the German tank nosed past it, followed by another tracked vehicle, camouflaged with foliage, carrying infantry. Behind them, the Germans set up an 88mm Flak gun. Both vehicles continued to move forward until they were 100 yards from the crossroads, at which point it became apparent that the tank was a PzKpfw IV. All this time, 4 Troop held their fire:

> 'At 0515hrs the enemy tank put up a flare and fired AP at the knocked-out tank, hitting it but not penetrating the front of the hull. Simultaneously the first shot was fired from the 17pr guard tank (LSgt Welsford MM) and his shot penetrated the front of the MkIV and blew the back of the turret out. The other 17pr joined in and, within a few seconds, the MkIV was blazing furiously with its turret blown clean off into the road beside it. Lt Martin (the Tp ldr) fired at the second veh and damaged it, blowing to pieces a considerable number

of Germans, many of them armed with bazookas. By this time the whole area was covered in dust, smoke and flames, and it was difficult to see anything. The enemy put up more flares and the 88mm began firing at the leaguer area. This was silenced effectively by the 17pr and the 105mm, which had moved up into a firing position. The 105mm engaged the area of the road beyond the 88mm and the troop-carrying veh, which limped away, was subsequently brewed-up further back. The two enemy tanks which had been on the flank must have hurried off in the semi-darkness during the engagement, as they were not found in the morning and they made no attempt to fire at the Sqn.'

Luckily for 4 Troop, the Germans made no further attempt to reach Bondeno that day.[6]

The following day, schwere Panzer-Abteilung 504, having rescued some paratroopers near Finale Emilia, pulled back to the Po River, where they destroyed their last seven Tigers before crossing to the north bank. Before this happened, though, one of their number took part in perhaps one of the strangest encounters of the entire campaign. This occurred near the town of Po di Volano, as described by Lieutenant Brian Harpur of 1 Kensington Regiment, the support battalion of the 78th Infantry Division:

'I awoke at dawn very bleary-eyed and walked forward from my jeep leaving my batman and driver behind. Having gone about a hundred yards in search of what I thought was one of my platoon areas, I suddenly realized that I was surrounded by the thick morning mist. I stood alone in order to take stock and to work out how I was going to find my way back. Suddenly the unmistakable metallic sound of tank tracks coming towards me could be heard. I stepped forward confidently to meet it because the previous night our own tanks had been all around us. I felt sure that this one was just an early riser like myself probably looking for a place for a nice brew-up of that beloved army beverage – hot tea laced with sweet condensed milk. As I waited in the middle of the road the comforting sound of tracks grew louder and louder. This was obviously a very big tank indeed. Probably one of our Shermans I reflected. Suddenly the mist parted and the terrific shape of a 60-ton Tiger burst upon me. A young German officer, his head above the turret, was speaking very quietly into his "inter-com" line to his crew below. The tank ground to a sudden halt. I found myself gazing down the muzzle of the longest and most viscous looking gun I have ever seen. … I looked at the German officer and he looked at me. We were both dumbfounded. …

'Frankly I was paralysed. Panic must have prompted me to make an instinctive reflex, which doubtless was sown in my subconscious mind through endless drills on some distant and long-forgotten parade ground. I solemnly unbuttoned my holster and drew my pistol! … He looked at me with almost a hint of amusement as I struggled with my pistol. He then pointed down at his big gun with the index finger of his right hand. He was obviously making it clear that a Smith & Weston .38 calibre pistol versus an 88mm high velocity gun was simply no contest. To emphasise the point he raised the same index finger and wagged it at me from right to left several times in the same way a parent admonishes a naughty child. It stood there transfixed. This was not the war I had heard so much about. I felt I should be killing someone or someone should be killing me. But no, this was ridiculous. It was the sort of situation dreamed up only in Charlie Chaplin movies. He then gave some instructions to his crew and the tank spun around and clanked away. As the mist started to envelop it my last glimpse of the German officer, with the distinct sense of humour, was as he turned round to give me a half salute. … I found myself waving back.'[7]

Once across the Po River, the end came quickly for schwere Panzer-Abteilung 504. Though they were able to pick up two repaired Tigers at San Pietro, both had to be abandoned and blown up on 22 April. The battalion eventually surrendered to American troops on 3 May in the Agordo Valley.

Chapter 11

ANALYSIS

British tank doctrine called for the main armament of both cruiser and infantry tanks to be an anti-tank gun. While this made sense for the former, as their role was to engage and defeat enemy armour, it seemed less so for the infantry tanks. This was because British military doctrine called for the artillery to provide fire support to the infantry, while the designated role of the infantry tank was to only protect infantry from enemy tanks, hence they only required an anti-tank gun. US doctrine was different – their tanks were not supposed to fight other tanks, which was the role of the tank destroyer. American tanks were, however, supplied with some AP rounds, for use only in the event that some enemy armour was encountered. Experience on the battlefield would soon reveal the fallacies of both doctrines.

The British started off the war with the 2-pdr anti-tank gun (40mm calibre) as their primary tank armament. At the time it was a perfectly adequate weapon, certainly one with better performance against armour than the main armament of the German PzKpfw III, the 37mm gun. Over time, this competitive edge started to slip as the Germans steadily up-gunned their PzKpfw III with a short, then a long 50mm main armament. At the same time, they steadily increased the armour on their tanks, and being face-hardened – with the surface of the armour plate of increased hardness to resist enemy projectiles – it easily broke up the solid shot of the British 2-pdr guns.

One thing German tanks did have was a high-explosive round for each tank gun, as did the Americans, who had both an HE and canister round for their 37mm guns. The British had developed such a round for the 2-pdr, but considered that it did not have sufficient explosive force to be effective. They did, however, have an HE round for their Bofors anti-aircraft gun, also 40mm in calibre, which was later fitted to a 2-pdr case and used with some success in the Pacific by New Zealand armoured forces, along with a canister round, using the US 37mm canister shell.

Unfortunately, the British were slow to replace the 2-pdr, being reluctant to interrupt its production at a time when they were rebuilding their armed forces after the heavy losses suffered in the battle for France in 1940. Nevertheless, they had been working on a replacement at the time, the 6-pdr, a field-mount version of it eventually being introduced during the first battle of Alamein in July 1942. Tank-mounted versions followed shortly afterwards, primarily on the Crusader Mk III, although six Churchill Mk IIIs were also trialled with 7 Motor Brigade at El Alamein. The timing was unfortunate for these new 6-pdr-armed tanks, as the battle also saw the debut of the US Sherman, which for the first time gave the British a turret-mounted 75mm gun firing both high explosive and armour-piercing rounds, their previous experience having been with the sponson-mounted 75mm of the Grant tank.

Even more unfortunate for their weapons development programme was that around this time, General Bernard Montgomery, commander of the Eighth Army in Egypt, went so far as to tell the British War Office that 'the 75mm is all we require'. This prompted the War Office to reverse its policy of working towards an anti-tank gun to outclass future tanks. Instead, the War Office reported: 'In view of the evidence to date, that the 75mm tank gun in use in American medium tanks is the best dual-purpose tank weapon yet produced, the 75mm should be adopted as soon as practicable as the main armament of the majority of British tanks.'[1] The net effect of this was to impose a further delay on Allied tank development and production in 1943.

Nevertheless, by the time the Eighth Army reached Tunisia, their latest anti-tank gun, the 17-pdr, had arrived, albeit on a field mount, debuting during the Battle of Medenine on 6 March 1943. This was followed in April by the introduction of an HE round for their 6-pdr anti-tank gun, effectively turning it into a dual-purpose weapon.[2] Sadly, it did not stop the replacement of this weapon in British tanks by their version of the US 75mm gun.

This was unfortunate for two reasons: the 6-pdr was better as an anti-tank weapon (future developments would improve this further) and may have been adequate in an infantry support role. In fact, Lieutenant Colonel E.V.M. Strickland, when he was commander of 145 Regiment, Royal Armoured Corps, in Italy in May 1943, maintained that the HE round of the 6-pdr gun was highly effective in comparison to that of the Sherman 75mm HE round, the latter tending to explode on branches of twigs.[3] It was also better as an anti-tank gun against the Tiger, Strickland noting:

> 'At a test held near Beja in May 1943, representatives of 18 Army Group proved this. The front of the turret of the German PZKW IV (Tiger) is approx. 102mm thick. The 6-pounder penetrated it at 300 yards – the 75mm could not penetrate it at 10 yards. Both guns will penetrate the sides and rear of the Tiger and all types of German Mk III and IV tanks at normal battle ranges.'[4]

Prime Minister Winston Churchill also had concerns about the British switch to the US 75mm gun, and on 23 April 1943 made this comment:

> 'I was not convinced in favour of the widespread adoption of the 75-mm gun, and a further meeting of the Defence Committee on this subject must take place before any decision is taken. … Reports from the Middle East Army are of great interest so far as tactical operations in the desert are concerned, and also generally. It must be remembered however that they have not seen the alternatives to the 75-mm gun. They have only very recently had any H.E. ammunition for the 6-pounder. They have never seen the 95-mm tank howitzer.'[5]

The trouble for the British was that by the end of the North African campaign, the Crusader had had its day as a combat tank and there was no replacement cruiser tank in sight for the foreseeable future. So whatever Churchill thought, the Sherman became the de facto cruiser tank. Later, in Italy, the Sherman even managed to infiltrate itself into the Churchill-equipped independent tank brigades, in the form of the Churchill NA75, a conversion made in Tunisia involving the fitting of a complete Sherman 75mm gun and mantlet to the Churchill Mk IV. Then, just prior to the launch of Operation Diadem at Cassino, each Churchill unit was issued with a squadron of Sherman tanks. Ironically, the 6-pdr tanks in these units were better equipped to deal with the Tiger than was the Sherman.

Fortunately, the British did not stop in their efforts to improve the performance of their anti-tank guns. Indeed, it was at this point in the continuation of the arms race that the path taken by the British and Germans started to diverge. The Germans had developed a tungsten-carbide core round for their tanks known as armour-piercing composite rigid (APCR), but shortages of tungsten forced them to focus on larger-calibre guns, longer barrels and high propellant charges, which culminated in the 128mm gun that was fitted to both the Maus and the Jagdtiger. They were the ultimate in behemoths, but their increased size placed limitations on where they could operate.

The British, while also looking at larger tanks, began to focus on ammunition. This eventually led to the development of the armour-piercing discarding sabot (APDS) round, the sabot being one component of a three-piece jacket wrapped around a central tungsten-iron core. These fell away when the round left the gun, giving it increased muzzle velocity – and hence penetration – as a result of its lighter weight and decreased wind resistance. It was less accurate than the German 88mm L/71 but had greater penetration.

APDS rounds were developed for both the 6-pdr and 17-pdr, these rounds first becoming available from March and July 1944 respectively. With the priority for this new ammunition going to units destined for the northwest European theatre of operations, Churchill tank units in Italy had to wait a little longer to receive the new APDS round. The first record of this comes from a report of some firing trials conducted at Riccione on 5 October 1944, when 6-pdr APDS rounds were fired at a brewed-up Tiger.[6] At least by then, the Sherman-equipped units had started to receive the 17-pdr version of the Sherman, though they may not have received their 17-pdr APDS rounds until April 1945, and then only on the basis of five rounds per tank in some units.[7] Nevertheless, until these technological improvements reached tank crews in Italy, they had to learn how to deal with the Tiger as best they could, particularly when calling down artillery or air strikes was not an option.

Although there were never enough Sherman 17-pdr tanks in Italy to deal with the heavier examples of German armour, there was still a place for the 75mm-armed Sherman as the higher velocity of the 17-pdr gun meant that often its HE round would bury itself too deep in the ground before exploding. The main requirement in Italy was fire support for infantry in attack or defence, and in that sense the 75mm gun was all they needed. According to veteran Eric Allsup, a subaltern in 8 Royal Tanks: 'The Sherman was a very good gun platform, you could put a round through a window or door and unlike artillery you could make it go through exactly the right place.'[8] Thus, it became the practice that 70 per cent of the ammunition rounds for the main gun were high explosive.

Of the two major strengths that the Tiger possessed, first and foremost was its powerful 88mm gun that could hit and penetrate Allied armour, particularly the Sherman, at long ranges and with a high degree of accuracy. The second strength was its armour protection, particularly its frontal armour that the Sherman could only penetrate at less than 100 metres. Examination of Tiger 211 at Massa Lombarda showed that it had been hit repeatedly on its vertical surfaces – up to twenty times – without any penetration. On its sides, Tigers were more vulnerable, particularly the lower side plates behind the road wheels. The one knocked out at Cecina was due to a penetration on the sponson itself at a distance believed to be only 25–30 metres.

On the other hand, the Tiger was plagued by mechanical issues, particularly its weak transmission, which while limiting its use in offensive operations, meant it was in its element when used in defence. It was here that Italy provided the ideal conditions, for instance the numerous small villages in the hills of Tuscany that mitigated against anything but a frontal approach. Conversely, the open plains of Anzio or the Po Valley prevented Allied armour from sneaking up on the Tiger from its more vulnerable sides, and when the rains came, such approaches became impossible as attacks were confined to the roads.

What worked against the Tigers was their tendency to operate alone, sometimes without even infantry support. This would have left a Tiger crew feeling quite vulnerable. Under such circumstances, it is not surprising that Allied tank crews had only to bounce a few armour-piercing shells off the hide of a Tiger to force it to disengage and turn around, as Cross did at Il Pino. This probably explains why Heberer and his crew were so willing to surrender to New Zealand infantry at La Romola. Likewise, the two Tigers near Prata, lacking infantry support, were easily unsettled when they came under fire from Howze's men.

One of the more interesting early campaign developments by New Zealand tank crews was the use of smoke, in particular one type of smoke shell. At that stage of the war, the British smoke shells used an allotrope of phosphorus, known as white phosphorus. This particular chemical is pyrophoric, self-igniting on contact with air and burns fiercely to produce a blanket of white phosphorus pentoxide vapour. For that reason, it was useful for marking enemy positions or masking friendly movement. It also had the capability of igniting cloth, fuel, ammunition and other combustibles, while it could cause severe burns on contact with skin and eyes and respiratory tract irritation.

At the request of the British, the Americans began developing a second type of smoke shell that eventually entered service as the M89, more popularly known as 'American' or 'Yank' smoke in British and Commonwealth service. This particular round used a mixture of roughly equal parts of hexachloroethane and zinc oxide, of which approximately 6 per cent was granular aluminium. Unlike white phosphorus, which created heat while burning and dissipating upwards, this alternative hugged the ground to produce an obscuring blanket.

There was another issue with the M89 smoke shell, namely its potential pulmonary toxicity, or effect on the lungs. However, for Allied tank crews facing a tank for which their armour-piercing round was ineffective, this was not a major issue. In a report highly critical of US armour, one comment from a veteran tank commander stands out: 'Our smoke shell is very good on any target, and I have found the Germans do not like it.'

In the case of the Tiger, as well as the obvious points of air ingress such as the mantlet or turret ring, none of the roof hatches could be sealed to airtightness. The loader's hatch had a fitting to lock it closed but with a small gap to allow fresh air in or out. The turret roof extractor fan was not sealed either, and was only on when firing the weapons, so air would enter or exit when it was switched on. Thus, with the Tiger not completely airtight, smoke from the M89 could easily penetrate inside and take some time to dissipate inside, sometimes to the detriment of its crew.

New Zealand crews quickly discovered the effectiveness of the M89 shell in their encounter with a Tiger at Villa Bonazza and used it successfully several times later, notably by Lieutenant Colmore-Williams at Sant'Andrea and by Sergeant Armstrong at Massa Lombarda. Of note in the latter engagement was that in Armstrong's tank, six of the fifteen rounds in the ammunition rack ring in the turret were American smoke. Of the rest, two were AP and the other seven APHE. This astonishingly high proportion of readily available smoke shells in the turret in a combat situation suggested the intention to use the M89 round offensively.

Nevertheless, the Tiger remained a major psychological obstacle for Allied tank crews in Italy, leading to cases of reporting Tigers where only PzKpfw IVs and StuG IIIs were involved – known as 'Tiger fear' – which in turn led to the misreporting of events afterwards in newspapers back home in New Zealand. Such was the case in one account in the *Waikato Times* on 31 July 1944 of the battle for San Michele, where the only armour met were PzKpfw IVs and StuG IIIs:

> 'A second thrust was more dangerous. It came from high ground around the little village of San Michele and was closely supported by tanks – both Mark 4 specials and Tigers. One of our companies was completely isolated without support weapons, but held its ground while German troops pressed in. Both the threatened New Zealand formations stood firm against the weight of the enemy's metal and by 10 o'clock the force of the drive had expended itself.'[9]

One New Zealand official unit historian, writing about the division's operations in Tuscany, summed it up as follows:

> 'The most striking point about this campaign was the moral effect of the Tiger tank. Unless the cards all turned in its favour a Sherman was no match for a Tiger, twice its size and armed with a gun that made the "seventy-five" look like a pop-gun. From the moment the Tiger appeared it became a kind of bogey, and the air was full of rumours of more and more Tigers lying in wait just ahead; just as in the desert every German gun was an "eighty-eight", so here

every tracked vehicle heard over in German territory was a Tiger. The natural result was that, quite suddenly, the New Zealand tanks became more cautious than they had ever been before. You could not blame the tankies, who were acting under divisional orders not to "stick their necks out". But to the infantry, who did not realise the length of the odds, and who had come to admire the Shermans for their willingness to tackle anything, the change was puzzling and disappointing. Infantrymen were apt to think unkind thoughts about the tankies' new caution; tankies to feel that the infantry was unreasonable and expected far too much of them. The high mutual regard of New Zealand tanks and infantry was in danger.'[10]

Appendix 1

VEHICLE DATA SHEETS

Sherman III	
Dimensions	
Length	5.84 metres
Width	2.62 metres
Height	2.74 metres
Weight	33 tonnes
Crew	5 (commander, gunner, loader, driver, spare driver)
Armour	
Hull	
Front upper	63.5mm at 47°
Front lower	108–50.8mm at 0–56°
Side	38mm at 0°
Rear	38mm at 10–12°
Top	19mm at 90°
Turret	
Mantlet	89mm at 0°
Front	76mm at 30°
Side	51mm at 5°
Rear	51mm at 0°
Top	25mm at 90°
Armament	
Main	75mm gun M3 in M34 mantlet
Secondary	.30 calibre M1919A4 co-axial in turret
Hull	.30 calibre M1919A4 bow mount

Sherman III	
Traverse	Hydraulic and manual
Ammunition	
75mm	97 rounds
.30 calibre	4,750 rounds
.45 calibre	600 rounds
Hand grenades	12
Engine	General Motors twin in-line diesel 280kw at 2,100rpm
Transmission	Spicer synchromesh, 5 forward, 1 reverse
Suspension	Vertical volute suspension
Performance	
Fuel capacity	522 litres
Operational range	241km
Maximum speed	40km/h
Maximum grade	60 per cent
Maximum trench	2,286mm
Maximum vertical wall	609mm
Maximum fording depth	1,016mm
Maximum turning circle	44.3 metres

Tiger 1	
Dimensions	
Length	6.2 metres
Length with gun	8.23 metres
Width	3.35 metres
Height	2.88 metres
Track width	724mm
Weight	50.8 tonnes
Crew	5 (commander, gunner, loader, driver, radio operator)
Armour	
Superstructure	
Front	102mm at 10°
Sides	82mm at 0°

Tiger 1	
Rear	82mm at 10°
Top	26mm at 0°
Hull	
Upper nose plate	102mm at 20°
Lower nose plate	62mm at 60°
Glacis plate	62mm at 80°
Sides	62mm at 0°
Rear	82mm at 20°
Floor	26mm at 90°
Turret	
Mantlet	97mm at 10°
Side	82mm at 0°
Rear	82mm at 0°
Top	26mm at 90°
Armament	
Main	88mm KwK 36 L/56 (elevation +10°, -9°)
Secondary	7.92mm co-axial
Hull	7.92mm hull
Traverse	Hydraulic
Ammunition	
88mm	92 rounds
7.92 calibre	5,700 rounds
Engine	Maybach HL230 P45 V12 (790 PS)
Transmission	Maybach Olvar preselect (8 forward, 4 reverse)
Suspension	Torsion bar, interleaved roadwheels
Performance	
Fuel capacity	540 litres
Operational range	195km
Maximum speed	45.4km/h
Maximum grade	30°
Maximum trench	3,960mm
Maximum fording depth	1,219mm

Appendix 2

COMPARATIVE GUN PENETRATIONS (IN MM)

Gun/Range	100	500	1,000	1,500	2,000
6-pdr AP	135	112	89	70	55
6-pdr APCBC	115	103	90	78	68
6-pdr APDS	177	160	140	123	108
75mm M72 AP	88	78	67	57	49
75mm M61 APCBC	101	90	78	68	59
76mm M7 APC M62	/	93	88	82	75
76mm M7 AP M79	132	109	135	116	64
76mm M7 HVAP M93	239	157	135	116	98
17-pdr AP	200	175	147	124	105
17-pdr APDS	275	256	233	213	194
75mm KwK 40 L/48 PzGr Ptr 39	110	97	86	75	64
75mm KwK 40 L/48 PzGr Ptr 40	143	120	97	77	/
88mm L/56 PzGr 39	132	110	99	91	83
88mm L/56 APCBC	171	130	119	109	99
88mm L/71 PzGr 39	203	185	165	148	132
88mm L/71 PzGr 40/43	237	217	193	171	153

Note: Range is in metres.

SOURCES

Archives New Zealand

WAII 1, DA 50/15/5, account by Shirley Hodson.
WAII, DA 48/1/34-71, 18 NZ Armoured Regiment, Oct 42–Nov 45.
WAII, DA 49/1/34-70, 19 NZ Armoured Regiment, Oct 42–Oct 45.
WAII, DA 50/1/34-71, 20 NZ Armoured Regiment, Oct 42–Nov 45.
WAII, DA 62/1/57, 26 Battalion, Apr 45.

Papers Past

Battle for Florence, *Waikato Times*, Volume 195, Issue 22414, 31 July 1944, p.4.

Personal Accounts

Ron Biggs – account by Ron Biggs of the Battle of Massa Lombarda on 12 April 1945.
Alan Burgess and Pat Stack, interview, 9 February 1999.
Doug Bull, interview, 1999.
Ray Curry, interview with Brendon O'Carroll, 16 November 1998.
Berthold Dölle – account by Berthold Dölle about his employment as a soldier during Second World War, 31 August 2001.
Rae Familton, interview, 30 December 2000.
Bill French, Ivan Hamilton, Arthur McNeil and Nigel Overton, interview, 26 November 1999.

Bruce Grainger, interview, 7 June 2000.
Syd Hemsley – interview, May 2001.
Friedrich Huhle – correspondence, 2000–2008.
Graeme Innes, interview, 14 March 1999.
Fritz Kessel – report of Oberfeldwebel Kessel, 2./sPtAbt 504, on 12 April 1945 at Massa Lombarda.
Lindsay McCully – interview with Colin Smith, Pukekohe, 30 July 2000.

National Archives, UK

48th Bn Royal Tank Regiment War Diary, September 1944, Appendix B, 13 Sept to 23 Sept 1944.

US Archives

846.9 After Action Report 751st Tank Bn, Mar 43–May 45.
847.31 After Action Report 701st Tank Destroyer Bn, Mar 42–Apr 45.
R-491702 Mud, Mountains and Armour, The 1st Armored Division from Rome to the Alps, A Research Report Prepared by Committee 17, Officers Advanced Course, The Armored School, 1948–1949. Fort Knox, Kentucky, 1949.

Articles

Holt, Robert and Guglielmi, Daniele, 'The Battle for Cecina', in *After the Battle* (London: Battle of Britain International Ltd, 2001), pp.30–37.

Books

Burdon, D.M., *24 Battalion* (Wellington: War History Branch, Department of Internal Affairs, 1953).
Chamberlain, Peter and Doyle, Hilary, *Encyclopedia of German Tanks of World War II* (London: Arms and Armour Press, 1978).

Cody, Joseph F., *28 (Māori) Battalion* (Wellington: War History Branch, Department of Internal Affairs, 1956).

Cody, Joseph F., *New Zealand Engineers, Middle East* (Wellington: War History Branch, Department of Internal Affairs, 1961).

Cooke, Peter, *Warrior Craftsmen. Royal New Zealand Electrical and Mechanical Engineers, 1942–1996* (Wellington: Defence of NZ Study Group, 2016).

Cooper, Belton Y., *Death Traps. The Survival of an American Armored Division in World War II* (New York: Ballantyne Books, 1998).

Dawson, William D., *18 Battalion and Armoured Regiment* (Wellington: War History Branch, Department of Internal Affairs, 1961).

Documents Relating to New Zealand's Participation in the Second World War 1939–45: Volume II (Wellington: Government Printer, 1951).

Doyle, Hilary and Jentz, Tom, *Panzerkampfwagen IV Ausf G, H and J. 1942–45. New Vanguard No. 39* (Oxford: Osprey Publishing, 2001).

Fletcher, David, *The Great Tank Scandal. British Armour in the Second World War. Part 1* (London: Her Majesty's Stationery Office, 1989).

Fletcher, David, *Tiger! The Tiger Tank: A British View* (London: HMSO Books, 1986).

Forczyk, Robert, *Desert Armour, Tank Warfare in North Africa. Gazala to Tunisia 1942–43* (Oxford: Osprey Publishing, 2023).

Guderian, Heinz, *Panzer Leader* (London: Michael Joseph, 1952).

Guglielmi, Daniele and Pieri, Mario, *Italienfeldzug. German Tanks and Vehicles 1943–1945* (AMMO of Mig Jiménez S.L., 2019).

Harpur, Brian, *The Impossible Victory. A Personal Account of the Battle for the River Po* (London: William Kimber & Co, 1980).

Henderson, Jim, *22 Battalion* (Wellington: War History Branch, Department of Internal Affairs, 1958).

Hirlinger, Kurt, *The Combat History of schwere Panzer-Abteilung 508* (Winnipeg: J.J. Fedorowicz Publishing, 2001).

Howe, George F., *The Battle History of the 1st Armored Division 'Old Ironsides'* (Uptown Station, TN: The Battery Press Inc, 1954).

Hunnicutt, Richard P., *Sherman. A History of the American Medium Tank* (Novato, CA: Presidio Press, 1978).

Jentz, Thomas L., *Panzertruppen. The Complete Guide to the Creation & Combat Employment of Germany's Tank Force, 1939–1942* (Atglen, PA: Schiffer Military History, 1996).

Kay, Robin, *Italy, Volume II. From Cassino to Trieste* (Wellington: War History Branch, Department of Internal Affairs, 1967).

Kershaw, Robert, *Tank Men. The Human Story of Tanks at War* (London: Hodder & Stoughton, 2009.)

Kleine, Egon and Kühn, Volkmar, *Tiger. The History of a Legendary Weapon, 1942–45* (Winnipeg: J.J. Fedorowicz Publishing, 1989).

Loughnan, Robert J.M., *Divisional Cavalry* (Wellington: War History Branch, Department of Internal Affairs, 1963).

Martin, George W., *Cassino to the River Po. Italy, 1944–45. A personal account of life and action in a tank troop* (G.W. Martin, 1999).

Münch, Karlheinz, *Combat History of schwere Panzerjäger-Abteilung 653* (Winnipeg: J.J. Fedorowicz Publishing, 1997).

Murphy, Walter E., *2nd New Zealand Divisional Artillery* (Wellington: War History Branch, Department of Internal Affairs, 1966).

Norton, Fraser D., *26 Battalion* (Wellington: War History Branch, Department of Internal Affairs, 1952).

Perrett, Bryan, *Panzerkampfwagen III. Medium Tank 1936–44. New Vanguard No. 27* (Oxford: Osprey Publishing, 1999).

Plowman, Jeffrey, *Rampant Dragons. New Zealanders in Armour in World War II* (Christchurch: John Douglas Publishing, 2014).

Pringle, David J.C. and Glue, W.A., *20 Battalion and Armoured Regiment* (Wellington: War History Branch, Department of Internal Affairs, 1957).

Pugsley, Christopher, *A Bloody Road Home. World War Two and New Zealand's Heroic Second Division* (New Zealand: Penguin Random House, 2014).

Puttick, Lieutenant General Sir Ernest, *25 Battalion* (Wellington: War History Branch, Department of Internal Affairs, 1960).

Ross, Angus, *23 Battalion* (Wellington: War History Branch, Department of Internal Affairs, 1959).

Schneider, Wolfgang, *Tigers in Combat I* (Winnipeg: Stackpole Books, J.J. Fedorowicz Publishing, 2000).

Sinclair, Don W., *19 Battalion and Armoured Regiment* (Wellington: War History Branch, Department of Internal Affairs, 1954).

Urbank, Axel and Becker, Hans, *Als Panzermann in Afrika und Italien 1942–45. Panzer Regiment 8 und schwere Panzer-Abt. 508* (Germany: Luftfahrverlag Start, 2013).

Zaloga, Steven J., *T-34/76 Medium Tank 1941–45. New Vanguard No. 9* (Oxford: Osprey Publishing, 1994).
Zaloga, Steven J. and Grandsen, James, *Soviet Heavy Tanks* (Oxford: Osprey Publishing, 1981).
Zuehlke, Mark, *The Gothic Line. Canada's Month of Hell in World War II Italy* (British Columbia: Douglas & McIntyre, 2013).
Zuehlke, Mark, *The River Battles. Canada's Month of Hell in World War II Italy* (British Columbia: Douglas & McIntyre, 2013).

The Tank Museum Bovington

48th Bn Royal Tank Regiment War Diary, September 1944.
2nd Lothians and Border Horse War Diary, April 1945.

ENDNOTES

Chapter 1: Tiger vs Sherman

1. Guderian, H., *Panzer Leader* (Michael Joseph, London, 1952), p.84.
2. Zaloga, S. J. and Grandsen, J., *Soviet Heavy Tanks* (Osprey Publishing, Oxford, 1981), p.3.
3. Zaloga, S., *T-34/76 Medium Tank 1941–45, New Vanguard No. 9* (Osprey Publishing, Oxford, 1994), p.11.
4. Kershaw, Robert, *Tank Men. The Human Story of Tanks at War* (Hodder & Stroughton, London, 2009), pp.199–200.
5. *Ibid.*, p.12.
6. Deighton, L., *Blitzkreig. From the Rise and Fall of Hitler to the Fall of Dunkirk.* (Book Club Associates, London, 1979), p. 151.
7. Fletcher, D., *The Great Tank Scandal. British Armour in the Second World War. Part 1* (Her Majesty's Stationery Office, London, 1989), p.3.
8. *Ibid.*, p.13.
9. Cooke, Peter, *Warrior Craftsmen. Royal New Zealand Electrical and Mechanical Engineers, 1942–1996* (Defence of NZ Study Group, Wellington, 2016), pp.128–129.
10. Hunnicutt, R.P., *Sherman. A History of the American Medium Tank* (Presidio Press, Novato, 1978), p.93.
11. Hunnicutt, p.525.
12. Cooper, Belton Y., *Death Traps. The Survival of an American Armored Division in World War II* (Ballantyne Books, New York, 1998), pp.25–28.

Chapter 2: Anzio to Rome

1. Urbank, Axel and Becker, Hans, *Als Panzermann in Afrika und Italien 1942–45. Panzer Regiment 8 und schwere Panzer-Abt. 508* (Luftfahrverlag Start, 2013), pp.149–150.
2. Hirlinger, Kurt, *The Combat History of schwere Panzer-Abteilung 508* (J.J. Fedorowicz Publishing, Winnipeg, 2001), p.34.
3. Hirlinger, p.34.
4. 846.9 After Action Report 751st Tank Bn, Mar 43–May 45.
5. Münch, Karlheinz, *Combat History of schwere Panzerjäger-Abteilung 653* (J.J. Fedorowicz Publishing, Winnipeg, 1997), p.267.
6. *Ibid.*, p.267.
7. Hirlinger, p.35.
8. Hirlinger, p.35.
9. Münch, p.270.

Chapter 3: The Cecina Tiger

1. Schneider, Wolfgang, *Tigers in Combat I* (Stackpole Books, J.J. Fedorowicz Publishing, Winnipeg, 2000), p.197; R-491702 Mud, Mountains and Armour, The 1st Armored Division from Rome to the Alps, A Research Report Prepared by Committee 17, Officers Advanced Course, The Armored School, 1948–1949 (Fort Knox, Kentucky, 1949), pp.42–43.
2. Howe, George F., *The Battle History of the 1st Armored Division 'Old Ironsides'* (The Battery Press Inc, Uptown Station, 1954), p.358.
3. *Ibid.*, p.359.
4. Holt, Robert and Guglielmi, Daniele, *The Battle for Cecina* (*After the Battle*) (Battle of Britain International Ltd, London, 2001), pp.33–34.
5. *Ibid.*, p.34.

Chapter 4: Encounter at Villa Bonazza

1. Ray Curry interview, 16 November 1998.

2. WAII, DA 48/1/34-71, 18 NZ Armoured Regiment. Oct 42–Nov 45, Summary of Sqn Operations From 22 Jul to 25 Jul 44.
3. Dawson, W.D., *18 Battalion and Armoured Regiment* (War History Branch, Department of Internal Affairs, Wellington, 1961), p.507.
4. *Ibid.*, pp.507–508.
5. Ray Curry interview, 16 November 1998.
6. Hirlinger, Kurt, *The Combat History of schwere Panzer-Abteilung 508* (J.J. Fedorowicz Publishing, Winnipeg, 2001) p.36.
7. Dawson, W.D., *18 Battalion and Armoured Regiment* (War History Branch, Department of Internal Affairs, Wellington, 1961), p.508.
8. *Ibid.*, p.509.
9. *Ibid.*, p.509.
10. Ray Curry.
11. Dawson, *18 Battalion*, pp.500–510.
12. Doug Bull interview, 1999.
13. Kelly Forest-Brown interview, 15 March 1999.

Chapter 5: The Tiger of La Romola

1. Rae Familton interview, 30 December 2000.
2. Pringle, D.J.C. and Glue, W.A., *20 Battalion and Armoured Regiment* (War History Branch, Department of Internal Affairs, Wellington, 1957), p.450.
3. *Ibid.,* p.451.
4. *Ibid.*, p.452.
5. Rae Familton interview, 30 December 2000.
6. Pringle and Glue, *20 Battalion*, p.452.
7. *Ibid.*, p.455.
8. Henderson, J., *22 Battalion* (War History Branch, Department of Internal Affairs, Wellington, 1958), pp.324–325.
9. Hirlinger, Kurt, *The Combat History of schwere Panzer-Abteilung 508* (J.J. Fedorowicz Publishing, Winnipeg, 2001), p.75.
10. Henderson, *22 Battalion*, p.325.

Chapter 6: The Road to Florence

1. Pringle, D.J.C. and Glue, W.A., *20 Battalion and Armoured Regiment* (War History Branch, Department of Internal Affairs, Wellington, 1957), p.457.
2. *Ibid.*, p.460.
3. Bill French interview, 26 November 1999.
4. Pat Stack interview, 9 February 1999.
5. Pringle and Glue, *20 Battalion*, p.466.
6. Murphy, W.E., *2nd New Zealand Divisional Artillery* (War History Branch, Department of Internal Affairs, Wellington), pp.632–663.
7. Graeme Innes interview, 14 March 1999.
8. *Ibid.*
9. Rae Familton interview, 30 December 2000.

Chapter 7: Tigers on the Adriatic

1. Zuehlke, Mark, *The Gothic Line. Canada's Month of Hell in World War II Italy* (Douglas & McIntyre, British Columbia, 2013), p.297.
2. *Ibid.*, p.297.
3. Ibid., p.446.
4. 48th Bn Royal Tank Regiment War Diary, September 1944, Appendix B 13 Sept to 23 Sept 1944.
5. Dawson, W.D., *18 Battalion and Armoured Regiment* (War History Branch, Department of Internal Affairs, Wellington, 1961), pp.557–558.
6. Pringle, D.J.C. and Glue, W.A., *20 Battalion and Armoured Regiment* (War History Branch, Department of Internal Affairs, Wellington, 1957), pp.497–498.
7. Zuehlke, Mark, *The River Battles. Canada's Month of Hell in World War II Italy* (Douglas & McIntyre, British Columbia, 2013), pp.59–61.
8. Zuehlke, Mark, *The River Battles*, pp.215–217.
9. Kay, Robin, *Italy Volume II. From Cassino to Trieste* (War History Branch, Department of Internal Affairs, Wellington, 1967), pp.279–284.
10. Martin, George W., *Cassino to the River Po. Italy 1944–45. A personal account of life and action in a tank troop* (G.W. Martin, 1999), p.95.

Chapter 8: Over the Senio River

1. Kay, R., *Italy Volume II. From Cassino to Trieste* (Historical Publications Branch, Department of Internal Affairs, Wellington), p.348.
2. Puttick, Lieutenant General Sir Edward, *25 Battalion* (War History Branch, Department of Internal Affairs, Wellington, 1960), pp.592–593.
3. Friedrich Huhle, notes.
4. Burdon, D.M., *24 Battalion* (War History Branch, Department of Internal Affairs, Wellington, 1953), p.318.
5. Burdon, *24 Battalion*, p.319.
6. Syd Hemsley interview, May 2001.

Chapter 9: Massa Lombarda

1. Cody, J.F., *28 (Maori) Battalion* (War History Branch, Department of Internal Affairs, Wellington, 1956), p.465.
2. *Ibid.*, p.466.
3. Ross, Angus, *23 Battalion* (War History Branch, Department of Internal Affairs, Wellington, 1959), p.448.
4. Dawson, W.D., *18 Battalion and Armoured Regiment* (War History Branch, Department of Internal Affairs, Wellington, 1961), p.621.
5. Puttick, Lieutenant General Sir Ernest, *25 Battalion* (War History Branch, Department of Internal Affairs, Wellington, 1960), p.450.
6. Cody, p.468.
7. Dawson, *18 Battalion*, p.623.
8. WAII, DA 62/1/57, 26 Battalion, April 45.
9. *Ibid.*
10. Lindsay McCully interview with Colin Smith, 30 July 2000.
11. Berthold Dölle – account by Berthold Dölle about his employment as a soldier during Second World War, 31 August 2001.
12. Fritz Kessel – report of Oberfeldwebel Kessel, 2./sPtAbt 504 on 12 April 1945 at Massa Lombarda.
13. Berthold Dölle.
14. Friedrich Huhle – personal account.
15. Ron Biggs – account by Ron Biggs of the Battle of Massa Lombarda on the12 April 1945.

16. Fritz Kessel.
17. Berthold Dölle.
18. Friedrich Huhle account.
19. Lindsay McCully.
20. WAII 1, DA 50/15/5, Shirley Hodson's account.
21. Fritz Kessel.
22. WAII 1, DA 50/15/5.
23. Bruce Grainger interview, 7 June 2000.
24. WAII 1, DA 50/15/5.
25. Pringle, D.J.C. and Glue, W.A., *20 Battalion and Armoured Regiment* (War History Branch, Department of Internal Affairs, Wellington, 1957), p.564.
26. Berthold Dölle account.
27. Lindsay McCully interview.
28. *Ibid.*
29. Berthold Dölle account.
30. WAII 1, DA 50/15/5.
31. Bruce Grainger interview.
32. Berthold Dölle account.
33. Cody, p.468.
34. Hans-Heinrich von der Gabelentz, personal account.
35. WAII 1, DA 50/15/5.
36. Horst Fahn account, 3 April 1974.
37. *Ibid.*
38. WAII 1, DA 50/15/5.
39. Lindsay McCully.
40. WAII 1, DA 50/15/5.
41. Lindsay McCully.
42. WAII 1, DA 50/15/5.
43. Lindsay McCully.
44. Friedrich Huhle.
45. Dawson, *18 Battalion*, pp.623–624.
46. Lindsay McCully.
47. Pringle, D.J.C., Glue, W.A. and Norton, F.D., *26 Battalion* (War History Branch, Department of Internal Affairs, Wellington, 1952), p.506; Kay, Robin, *Italy Volume II. From Cassino to Trieste* (War History Branch, Department of Internal Affairs, Wellington, 1967), p.440.

Chapter 10: Final Days

1. 2nd Lothians and Border Horse War Diary, 19 Apr 45.
2. Martin, George W., *Cassino to the River Po. Italy 1944–45. A personal account of life and action in a tank troop* (G.W. Martin, 1999), p.104.
3. *Ibid.*, p.104.
4. 2nd Lothians and Border Horse War Diary, 1945, C Sqn – Advance to Bondeno 22 Apr 45.
5. *Ibid.*, B Sqn 2 Lothians. Enemy Counter-attack and its Defeat – Bondeno Area am 23 Apr 45.
6. Schneider, Wolfgang, *Tigers in Combat I* (Stackpole Books, J.J. Fedorowicz Publishing, Winnipeg, 2000), p.203.
7. Harpur, B., *The Impossible Victory. A Personal Account of the Battle for the River Po* (William Kimber & Co, London, 1980).

Chapter 11: Analysis

1. Kershaw, Robert, *Tank Men. The Human Story of Tanks at War* (Hodder & Stroughton, London, 2009), p.234.
2. Churchill Minutes on Tank Supply 23 April 1943, Appendix C, Part 1.
3. Strickland lecture to 145 RAC on 24 April 1944.
4. *Ibid.*
5. Churchill Minutes on Tank Supply 23 April 1943, Appendix C, Part 1.
6. WO.170/858 12 Battalion Royal Tank Regiment War Diary, October 1944.
7. Graeme Innes interview, 14 March 1999.
8. Kershaw, *Tank Men*, p.282.
9. Papers Past. 'Battle for Florence', *Waikato Times*, Volume 195, Issue 22414, 31 July 1944, p.4.
10. Dawson, W.D., *18 Battalion and Armoured Regiment* (War History Branch, Department of Internal Affairs, Wellington, 1961), p.521.